"While the apparent goal of the narrative is ⸻
world's largest malls, Gremaud's journey is ⸻
globalization, income inequality, and the aⵑ ⸻
heritage as it is about shopping."

    —KAREN STERNHEIMER, University of Southern California

"We feel Gremaud's exhaustion as she crosses yet another time zone, entering another mega-mall where she is unlikely to see the light of day for hours or breathe fresh air. Her observations of her fellow travellers are razor sharp."

    —JONATHAN KAPLANSKY, literary translator

ALL THE WORLD'S A MALL

ALL THE
WORLD'S
A MALL

RINNY GREMAUD

TRANSLATED BY LUISE VON FLOTOW

 UNIVERSITY *of* **ALBERTA** PRESS

Published by

University of Alberta Press
1-16 Rutherford Library South
11204 89 Avenue NW
Edmonton, Alberta, Canada T6G 2J4
amiskwaciwâskahikan | Treaty 6 |
Métis Territory
uap.ualberta.ca | uapress@ualberta.ca

LIBRARY AND ARCHIVES CANADA
CATALOGUING IN PUBLICATION

Title: All the world's a mall / Rinny Gremaud ;
    translated by Luise von Flotow.
Other titles: Monde en toc. English
Names: Gremaud, Rinny, 1977– author. |
    von Flotow, Luise, 1951– translator.
Series: Wayfarer (Edmonton, Alta.)
Description: Series statement: Wayfarer |
    Translation of: Un monde en toc.
Identifiers: Canadiana (print) 20230237908 |
    Canadiana (ebook) 20230444849 |
    ISBN 9781772127126 (softcover) |
    ISBN 9781772127201 (EPUB) |
    ISBN 9781772127218 (PDF)
Subjects: LCSH: Gremaud, Rinny, 1977–
    —Travel. | LCSH: Shopping malls. | LCSH:
    Shopping malls—Social aspects. |
    LCSH: Shopping centers. | LCSH:
    Shopping centers—Social aspects. |
    LCSH: Consumption (Economics) | LCSH:
    Consumption (Economics)—Social
    aspects. | LCSH: Shopping. | LCSH:
    Shopping—Social aspects. |
    LCGFT: Travel writing.
Classification: LCC HC79.C6 G7413 2023 |
    DDC 306.3—dc23

First edition, first printing, 2023.
First printed and bound in Canada by
Houghton Boston Printers, Saskatoon,
Saskatchewan.
Copyediting by Audrey McClellan.
Proofreading by Mary Lou Roy.

University of Alberta Press is committed to
protecting our natural environment. As part
of our efforts, this book is printed on Enviro
Paper: it contains 100% post-consumer recycled fibres and is acid- and chlorine-free.

University of Alberta Press gratefully acknowl-
edges the support received for its publishing
program from the Government of Canada,
the Canada Council for the Arts, and the
Government of Alberta through the Alberta
Media Fund.

Published with the support of the Swiss Arts
Council Pro Helvetia.

For Pierre, Ulysse and Lucile

CONTENTS

TRANSLATOR'S NOTE

SINCE RINNY GREMAUD'S 2014 TRIP, some brands have changed names and/or owners, and corporate ownership has changed owing to sale, death, or malfeasance. The West Edmonton Mall roller coaster closed in January 2023. The last passenger flight to Atatürk Airport was in April 2019; by 2022, air cargo operations had moved to the new Istanbul Airport.

In January 2014, 1 euro was worth about 1.50 Canadian dollars.

ON MY WAY

GETTING READY TO TRAVEL. Folding up clothes for extreme
cold, for the tropics, and for conditioned air. A swimsuit and merino
wool leggings. Comfortable clothes for the hours I'll be spending
in airplanes. Business clothes for shaking hands with people in
suits and ties. Sturdy shoes and a jacket with lots of pockets for
long walks in industrial areas and along highways. I'm off on a tour
of the world. I am a journalist.

In my toiletries bag there's mild face soap, tonic lotion, cotton
balls, moisturizing gel, eye cream, day cream, anti-wrinkle night
cream, makeup base, makeup remover. In another small bag: an
eyeliner, an eyebrow pencil (with a little brush at the end), concealers,
a little compact with beige liquid foundation, mascara, tweezers,
blush, a light lipstick. I am a woman, almost forty years old.

On the station platform, a little boy and his father have come
to say goodbye. My son and the man I love. Every day of the year,
ever since they came into my life, I think about them like I think
about myself, or rather, instead of myself. I forget myself. Love as
alienation. They are my most important investment, the best, the
most difficult. They are the sum total of my sacrifices. The train
moves off. Travelling, running away.

I know my way around Geneva airport: there's a sidewalk that
leads from the train station to the check-in; it runs along the

parking lot and is painted in yellow stripes, with the asphalt alter-natingly smooth and rough. I know by heart the sound the wheels of my suitcase will make at this point, suddenly taking on a binary rhythm, rough, smooth, rough, smooth, "rrr," "sss," "rrr," "sss"—that lasts less than thirty seconds, just enough time to move from one interior to another and get a dash of cadenced fresh air. This is the precise moment when, through some mysterious synesthesia, I know I am on my way.

◌ In January 2014 I went on a tour of the world. Crossed all the time zones, one of them twice, heading west. I tried to adapt to five different settings without ever managing to do so: Edmonton, Beijing, Kuala Lumpur, Dubai, Casablanca, and then home. In less than a month, five of my days had far more than twenty-four hours. Somewhere over the north Pacific I lost an entire day in the mechanics of the meridians—it was a Saturday. There's a French expression, *être à l'ouest*, "to be in the west," meaning "to be spaced out." I spent twenty-three days in the west.

In this short stretch of time I travelled through fourteen airports, for a total of forty-two hours. I took off my boots and pulled the electronics out of my hand luggage for eighteen secu-rity checks—the differential is due to small cultural differences that persist despite extremely normed airport environments. I got on and off thirteen different airplanes. I spent around fifty-nine hours in pressurized cabins, my nostrils dry and my ankles swollen, at more than 10,000 metres altitude, dozing off in front of some awful screen in an always-the-same entertainment console, framed above a folding table. I accumulated 23,800 miles on my frequent flier card, the equivalent of 38,300 kilometres of air travel.

I went on a tour of the world, and before I left, people remarked on how exotic my waypoints were. I was, after all, going to three different continents. I would face extreme climates—minus 23 Celsius in Alberta and plus 31 Celsius in Malaysia; encounter various religions; and operate in five different languages. With anxious exclamation marks in their voices they wished me *bon voyage* and lots of fun. I didn't have any fun, and for good reason: I was on a tour of the world's biggest shopping centres, with constant air-conditioned temperatures of 21 degrees Celsius.

Agreed, it was a strange idea. Because the right-minded folks of this world tend to concur that shopping centres are to be despised. They say that *malls*—pronounced "mawls" or "mals" or even "molls"—are sinister places, cultural and aesthetic deserts, where the dead souls of a population that has converted to the religion of consumerism mill around. They say, and secretly hope, that malls are business models on the verge of extinction, dinosaurs condemned to die by the rise of online shopping. They say that malls are the graveyards of local culture and the worst form of globalization. Basically, they all have their set opinions, and in industrialized francophone Europe the feeling seems to be that malls are not really a concern, at least not for the intellectuals, the aesthetes, the people who count, because these people shop in their local boutiques and delicatessens anyway. No one would dream of subjecting themselves to further research on the "mallification" of the world; it would just be too boring.

But the mall is neither as exotic nor as peripheral a place as one might hope. It concentrates the shopping street and reduces the city to its mercantile function. As a laboratory that presents or prefigures, the mall, in fact, creates a model of what is happening all around us, in all our city centres.

The mall is a microcosm of the world. In its own way, it is a utopia.

LAUSANNE

I LIVE IN LAUSANNE, on the Swiss shores of Lake Geneva.
For as long as I can remember I have felt sad about how ugly this
city's streets are. I say this not to be snobbish but because I am
convinced that this ugliness is not relative. It's not because I have
seen much more beautiful streets that I find these ones particularly ugly. The streets of Lausanne, and in particular the streets
in the centre of Lausanne, are intrinsically ugly, even objectively
ugly. Since the 1970s the disastrous architectural and urban planning choices made in the city's development have constructed
a remarkably impoverished commercial landscape, a city centre
that is utterly hideous and so un-chic it is beyond repair. Which is
not to say that the ensemble is completely devoid of charm. But
walking through that part of the city I can't help but feel grumpy,
irritated by this constructed environment: it seems so final, so
irremediable.

I have always thought Lausanne was too small for me. I would
come back from my travels and be confronted by its ugliness.
This city that I love, and that I prefer to many others, would strike
me—on the world's scale—as filled with impossibilities and
small-mindedness. As though the lack of panache that I tend to
ascribe more generally to this part of Switzerland had materialized

in its buildings and was reflected in its shop windows. A poor city centre, poor pedestrian streets, a poor marketplace, with nothing more to offer than musty café-restaurants and drab stores.

Over the last decade I have observed a rather disconcerting phenomenon take hold in Lausanne: any shop that was empty would sooner or later become a shoe store. If a business closed down—a butcher shop, a chocolate shop, a fashion boutique, a gift/souvenir store, a hardware store, a bookstore, a fabric store, mobile telephones, housewares, fashion furniture, discount shops...whatever—in the next year a shoe store would open up. Even the shoe stores were replaced by shoe stores.

Invariably, mid-range stores would be selling low-quality shoes in a completely nondescript setup. Sometimes they were branches of well-known brands with outlets in all the other cities of Switzerland, or in all of Europe. But more often they were independent stores, the kind that employ one or two older Italian women and offer an assortment of shoes with medium high heels made in China.

I thought about researching this strange change in the urban landscape. Calling the commercial authorities and building managers, going door to door in the pedestrian streets to survey the neighbours. Not in order to understand why the other shops were failing, but to figure out what systemic anomaly was allowing shoe stores to proliferate the way they were—without ever really flourishing, however, since they too ended up disappearing.

As far as I know, the mid-range shoe business does not have massive profit margins. It is a sector that depends on the economic climate of a place. In times of crisis, this type of product tends to give way to less frequent purchases of high-quality items: when there is not much cash, a good pair of expensive, durable, and classic shoes is considered worth more than several pairs of fashion-dependent throwaways.

So from the perspective of economics, the proliferation of shoe stores was counterintuitive. Nor could it be explained by some local idiosyncrasy or twist in the market. Something about local business realities was allowing shoe stores to multiply.

I devised a number of hypotheses.

First: these stores were less important for selling shoes than they were for laundering the money of various underground economies. It is a known fact that small business offers the easiest ways for illicit money to become legal. Who would check if the money deposited in a bank by the owner of a shoe store actually came from the sale of shoes?

My second hypothesis was that given the same rental income, building managers would favour a shoe store as a tenant over any other type of business because it would require very little renovation, and so the lease agreement was simpler and less costly.

Third, I hypothesized that the countless regulations, sanitary rules, and other controls on business activities might discourage other businesses more than shoe stores. The Belgian owner of a clothing boutique that was established in the old city centre had talked to me at length about the frustration he felt at the treatment meted out by commercial authorities, who astounded him with their ball-busting policies. After five years in business and tired of the struggle, he closed his shop, for which he had had innovative renovation plans that didn't conform to regulations. It was replaced by a shoe store.

Finally, my fourth hypothesis: Lausanne is known worldwide for its three spectacular topographic levels, extending over three hills. The explanation for the glut of shoe stores could simply be technical: the city's paving stones destroy the shoes that trudge over them more quickly than the streets in other cities do. Of the four hypotheses, this was the simplest and the least likely. But resting as it did on the issue of demand, it was worth considering, if only formally.

Taken together, or one by one, these four avenues of research would doubtless have allowed me to break through the mystery of this proliferation. But the idea collected dust in a corner of my brain. Like so many other projects that are set aside for better days, this one ended up dissolving in my body; I metabolized it, digested and assimilated it until I developed the illusion that it had become a reality. This is the privilege of indecisiveness: the capacity to believe that there is but a short step between an idea and its realization, a step so negligible that it is quite useless to even take it.

And then, over time, things changed in Lausanne, for the better. A certain gentrification brought a new kind of commerce to some areas, a more targeted, independent, courageous commerce. On the other hand, a large number of bankrupted shoe stores were replaced by real estate agencies or the branches and outlets of global brands. Like anywhere else, these brands are the only ones that can and do take on long-term leases for stores located in busy city centres.

Over thirty years I have seen Lausanne exchange its local unsightliness for global unsightliness, which has turned it into a clone of neighbouring cities and all the other cities of the same size the world over. Lausanne, which felt too small for me yesterday, has become too global.

◌ It never ceases to amaze me how fatalistic people are about the ugly environments they live in. As though the daily suffering, the depressing, abrasive aggression that makes the body resist both passively and permanently, only really affected a handful of overly sensitive aesthetes with time on their hands, who could just move somewhere else since they generally belong to the well-heeled classes anyway. Let them go build architects' villas in the suburbs, or buy a loft in some gentrified neighbourhood, and stop filling our ears with complaints of privilege. The people have neither time nor money to bother with good taste.

Now, I'm not so concerned with taste, good or bad. I am concerned with the ugliness that takes over our pedestrian streets or city squares when these host nothing but franchises, low-end clothing chains, and branches of supermarkets. The uniformly garish windows, with the same global brands, ensconced at the foot of high-rises that have been constructed or renovated without style or spirit. I am concerned with the criminal lack of vision and originality that causes not-so-clever entrepreneurs, driven by imbecilic optimism, to keep opening franchises that only make building managers happy.

If only it were a question of taste. But the mediocre retailers are a symptom, much like the omnipresence of global brands. They are evidence of a system, a chain of irresponsibility, petty personal interests, cowardice, abandonment, an accumulation of indifference. I am referring to real estate developers who play up profitability, and to municipal authorities in charge of urban development who wash their hands of the question. I am referring to a kind of liberalism that hardly conceals its laissez-faire attitudes, and to the inhabitants of these tacky cities who hardly react.

Why is it that the commercial offerings of our city centres are not a political topic? We seldom hear that the urban environment plays a role in a citizen's well-being. And the reason we seldom hear it is that those who manipulate ideas don't want to touch unsavoury topics such as consumption or the buying and selling of real estate. Or if they do, it is only to denounce the subjugation and manipulation of the masses.

As far as I am concerned, the levelling of the commercial offerings in our cities has consequences that are quite concrete and reach beyond the sole, rather tainted, pleasure of the consumer. They touch the heart of a citizen's feeling of empowerment or weakness.

The commercial environment is an essential part of the physical reality we inhabit. If it no longer translates to a place and a community but only a system—the system of chains and franchises, a system that has nothing to do with us and ignores us, a system for which we are nothing and which is nothing to us—then it doesn't matter if we are here or somewhere else. Or nowhere, for that matter, on the web, in our pajamas, in bed.

Simultaneously, the feeling of what is possible erodes. Business, commercial activity, is reserved for a handful of big industrial groups. Doing business within and for a community, developing a local offering that is adapted to the needs of a particular population, has become a sort of abstraction, a model from another time.

So what is it that makes a place feel like home? What is it that anchors us, creates community and social connection and the urge to act on what surrounds us, or the feeling this is even possible? The urban landscapes that we move through, everything our eyes automatically take in, the streets we walk with our children, it all adds up. And if everything is ugly, uniformly ugly, then this limits our boldness and also our desires.

EDMONTON

ALBERTA IS AN ALMOST RECTANGULAR PROVINCE, set squarely into the grid between the 49th and 60th parallels of the Northern Hemisphere and the 120th and 110th western meridians, with a rather large slip of the pen marking the bottom left-hand side, where the topographer encountered the Rocky Mountains and drew a serrated edge into the geometric figure. Inside the rectangle are prairies, and winters to cut with a knife. If it were a country, this province of Canada would be somewhere between Qatar and Norway in terms of petrodollars per inhabitant. It has the world's largest tar sands, the new gold mines that crowds of migrants flock to. It is cold in Alberta, but there is little unemployment.

Cold: minus 23 degrees Celsius. While this figure excites TV commentators and the aficionados of weather reports, it means little for the body. The interiors, where human beings hole up in the winter, are overheated, with the result that you're in a constant sweat from wearing too many clothes.

I am at the lost-baggage counter of Edmonton airport, two hours into the haze of jet lag. About forty other dispossessed travellers are waiting in line; like me, they are suffering the effects of the airline chaos caused by a cold snap from the North Pole.

The media, with their sense of drama, are calling this a "polar vortex," like a plot device in a Roland Emmerich disaster movie, and in these early, empty, slow news days of January, this meteorological anomaly fills the airwaves.

The entire north of the continent has been paralyzed by snow and ice. Only one in every ten airplanes can take off, and in all the big airports, people are asleep, draped over their hand luggage in improvised campsites, the stench in the waiting areas increasing along with their resemblance to refugee camps. This spectacle of the tourist in pieces and the businessman run aground is moving, especially as everyone can see themselves reflected in the same mirror. Ever since the tourist condition has become hyper-democratized, airports have become familiar places for disasters to morph into fantasy. And hence, matter for the media.

To disburden the airports, the planes that are still flying take an overload of passengers. One result of this is that the contents of the cargo holds are proportionately reduced. A random selection of suitcases is unloaded before a flight takes off and waits as long as it takes for the next connection. All the while the lost-baggage counters are registering the lamentations of at least one third of the travellers.

In the line ahead of me is a young man, twenty-six years old, with dark skin and originally from India. He is wearing a hoodie and jeans. In some other place or in a movie he might be a computer programmer. Here, he is a mechanical engineer, on his way to Fort McMurray, a tar sands centre in the middle of the boreal forest where you can earn a six-figure salary without having finished high school, where alcohol and sex work are reputed to be rampant, where you work for two months and then go home for two months—home, or somewhere else. Alberta still has a bit of the Wild West.

Behind me are three men from New Brunswick. They are going to work in the tar sands too, and are a closer representation of how you might imagine a population of adventurers. Two of them are mountains of hairy flesh, thirtyish and looking worn from alcohol. They talk non-stop, or rather, they bellow. The third one is skinny, visibly older, late forties, with the leathery skin of the manual labourer, his gaze constantly shifting to the floor as though to apologize for being a bother, muttering the occasional uncertain word. They don't know each other, these three guys, but they're travelling together to a camp in the Cold Lake region, near the Saskatchewan border, for a new job they can't tell me anything about. Labourers, with no qualifications. And very annoyed at the loss of their baggage, which contains everything they need for the next months and their precious workboots. "No boots, no work," grunts one of the bearded men, irritated at the idea of losing a day's salary for some meteorological caprice.

There are no coincidences, only probabilities. In a province that is rich in hydrocarbons but low in population, and whose development is forcing it to siphon blue-collar labour from all over Canada and beyond, the people you meet at the airport belong to this class of intermittent oil workers. No one comes to Edmonton as a tourist. That's what the deputy director of the tourism office tells me two days later.

☼ A night taxi. Three-lane highway in the snow. There is heavy traffic in both directions, lots of trucks, pickups, four-wheel-drive vehicles. Windshield wipers fighting snowflakes, left, right, left, right. My suitcase is not in the trunk. I am arriving in Edmonton like a shipwreck survivor.

Along the way, nothing but the grey prairie huddling in the dead season. Time goes by at fifty miles an hour, the landscape doesn't move. The snowy flats go on and on in the headlights. My fatigue filters and slows the panorama to a crawl. A surge of thoughts, assorted dreams, unfurl before my open eyes.

When the taxi takes a sharp right turn, wild heart palpitations tear me out of my drowsiness. This is my hotel, opening its large automatic doors and damp carpet to me, located somewhere between a parking lot, a field of snow, and the oldest of America's megamalls.

☼ After a three-day journey from Europe, with unexpected layovers and polar contretemps, I have blown into one of the most spectacular North American happenings in the middle of nowhere. West Edmonton Mall stretches out over there, on the other side of the street, 493,000 square metres of it, the equivalent of sixty-eight soccer fields to put it in journalist-speak, just a little larger than the Vatican. I face it with incomprehensible excitement that feels like enthusiasm but is quite counterintuitive. I am contemplating one of those places on earth where absolute emptiness has been translated into concrete. Built to contain oversized leisure and retail activities.

Contrary to what one might imagine, West Edmonton Mall is not just a gigantic rectangular model of a shoe store. Built in four different stages and over fifteen years, it stretches out long and platitudinal, like a monstrous amberjack that has swallowed strange geometrical shapes. The stores are located on only two floors, but certain other attractions, such as the super slide in the waterpark, a huge figure-eight roller coaster with a triple loop, and the multiplex cinema, create huge protuberances on the back and the flanks of the building.

To really grasp the colossal size and expanse of this construct, which floats in an equally huge expanse of parking lots, you would have to study it from above, from a God's-eye perspective or a drone's. From my human perspective, which is also that of the customers it ingurgitates daily, such a perspective is impossible. The depth, the sheer size of the mall, remain virtual, although you are in its presence and moving about in its belly.

☼ The West Edmonton Mall Inn, where I am staying, has eighty-eight rooms and looks like any other suburban hotel on this continent: royal blue carpet, extra-low bathtubs that are twice the size of European ones, oversized beds for overweight clients. As its name indicates, only a pedestrian passage and the width of the north wing of the parking lot separate it from the mall itself.

Three nights, paid in advance. A magnetic card opens the door to my room on the second floor. The bathroom is to the right of the entrance, where I drop my small backpack under the main light switch—the pack containing everything I now own. To my left is a tea/coffee set on a small table screwed into the wall, with a pack of peanuts and another one of salted mini-pretzels. Below, a wastebasket. Farther on, the room extends and opens onto two queen-size beds that face a giant flat-screen television, a Korean LG brand. It presides over an imitation walnut buffet that contains a small safe.

I am not the right size nor do I have the right family setup to inhabit this space; the monstrous scale of the furniture is almost a reproach.

○ The big mirror in the bathroom, which takes up the entire width of the wall to the right of the door, reflects the familiar image of me as a solo traveller. An image I like because it erases the social me, the me that swindles. When I travel, I do not appear, I don't exist for anyone. Without makeup, I am a little girl with wrinkles. My bare face: small creases around my eyes, eyelids going limp, bluish circles under my eyes, blackheads on my nose, small spots, hairs, red marks, short lashes, dry lips, pallid, uneven skin.

Travelling solo means momentarily suspending the vain battle to maintain appearances and not giving a damn about being seen. No longer being a woman, a visible body, and becoming just eyes that are open to other people and the world. No longer dressing up, but simply covering yourself, making yourself invisible in func- tional, warm, comfortable clothing. Being nothing more than movement. To travel is to disappear.

⬭ An inventory of my equipment indicates survival strategies: besides the clothes I'm wearing I have my computer, my passport, a cardholder, a wallet, cables, a universal adapter, my cellphone, a file full of reports on commercial real estate, electronic air tickets and hotel reservations, some magazines and newspapers from yesterday, a U-shaped blow-up cushion, a pair of mitts and a hat, some hand cream, and "northern berry" lip balm. That's it.

It is 6 p.m. in Alberta, 2 a.m. according to the internal clock I left behind in Switzerland. I'd like to lie down, turn on the TV, connect to free Wi-Fi, check and zap a few unimportant emails, and fall asleep with an empty stomach, or fill it with peanuts. Travel is a struggle with yourself. I'm going to take that struggle outside. I'm going to do a bit of shopping.

⬭ I step into West Edmonton Mall at Bourbon Street, on the ground floor of the north wing. I enter a wide corridor lined with the façades of houses, its floor finished with fake paving stones, and the whole thing lit up with Paris-style street lamps whose light bulbs imitate little orange flames that, day or night, give the place the feel of a party about to start. There are restaurants left and right—a grill, an Italian place, a Mexican one, pubs, clubs, a piano bar—that produce stereotyped diversity, a standardized "mix," an offer that works: it satisfies 95 percent of customers' tastes.

The corridor is not very long. Part of it is under construction. Each place has its "terrace" that overlooks the "street" and is separated from the "inside" of the establishment by glass-less window frames. I am using quotation marks for where there are only empty signs, elements of the décor that cite the outside world in this entirely enclosed environment. Here it is always summer, there's a southern feel, a tinge of *la dolce vita*.

Bourbon Street, a reference to the renowned street in New Orleans, is one of three "themed" passages in this mall. In the centre of a room hung with velour at The Red Piano, a man wearing a tuxedo, his hair in a ponytail, is playing and singing "Candle in the Wind," not as well as Elton John. A few people, mainly couples, are seated at tables. At this hour, there's no crowd.

I reach what seems to be the mall's main thoroughfare, which I wander along, just to see. The lighting has turned white. The effect is daytime busy-ness in this long two-storey tunnel with its glass dome. The night and the freezing cold outside are mere abstractions, long-gone memories of an animal condition, an evolutionary moment when we still lived in a nychthemeral rhythm and climatic conditions we did not choose.

Everything here is at once familiar and unfamiliar, the store signs, the architectural codes, the behaviours, the goods and services. At the end of the broad avenue floats a 1:1 replica of Christopher Columbus's *Santa Maria.* A bridge allows you to cross the chlorinated turquoise water, edged with unreal rocks. People are taking selfies: a man in a striped pink polo shirt and an ageless woman in front of the fake boat.

The mall is relatively busy given the time and the day, 7 p.m. on a Thursday in January, the "post-Christmas" period that is reputedly dead for business. There's a strange background noise, fizzing fountains, footsteps slapping or squealing as the acoustics change with the height of the ceiling.

After a ten-minute walk I can tell that a change of scene is imminent: there's noise coming out of a domed space, an arena, sudden sporty shouts, the sound of a body thudding into a wall. It's a skating rink, with a hockey practice in full swing. Welcome to Canada. A large white net protects onlookers from uncontrolled sorties of the puck as they watch the show from the "terrace" of the "café" close by and sip large milky drinks from cardboard cups.

I skirt the rink, heading to the left, and turn left again to float along in a crowd until I reach a drab, almost deserted corridor with wedding gown and interior décor shops, all of them already closed. Finally there's a light ahead: the entrance to a big Target store, an American discount retailer whose Canadian division declared bankruptcy a year after my visit and closed more than half of its outlets, including this one.

I decide to buy what I need in order to keep operating for a day or two without my suitcase: a basic toiletries bag, some underwear, a T-shirt. No trousers. It would be risky to buy without trying them on, and I can't envisage taking my clothes off here in these low-cost neon-lit surroundings when my belly is aching for food and I'm low on energy. I'll buy a pair at H&M later on, because there's no doubt in my mind that the world's leader in fast fashion will also have planted its glorious flag in these northern precincts of the American continent, close to or at the very edge of its ancestral forests. I can buy a pair of trousers from this Swedish operation with my eyes closed. I know my size by heart. The ability to easily purchase a piece of clothing that is identical to something you've left hanging in your wardrobe 7,500 kilometres away is one of the strange and exasperating experiences that globalization offers us.

The Target store I am getting lost in is both enormous and empty. I wander around in search of an employee who might show me where the toothpaste is. No one seems to work in these low-cost places anymore, let alone in one going bankrupt. There are exactly ten times the number of employees per square metre in a Tiffany's jewellery store as in a Target—I've done the math. I end my visit scanning my purchases into one of a bank of twelve self-serve cash registers, under the indifferent gaze of the sole South Asian employee, who I suspect is underpaid. In the world of hard discount retail, the losses incurred by someone occasionally "forgetting" to pay are much lower than the cost of hiring a real human being, even in perfectly demeaning conditions.

◌ By 9 p.m., Edmonton time, my body has spent one night without sleep and I feel like I'm reliving certain early mornings of my teenage years when I attended punk concerts in distant corners of Switzerland, earning tinnitus from the 115-decibel noise and a blank brain from having drunk too much. After those concerts we had to kill the hours between the club closing and the first morning train home, walking through sleeping cities, our bodies heavy, verging on comatose, with no other ambition than to stay upright, survive the next minute, and the next, and the one after that. Feeling cold right to our innards, our feet raw in shoes that had become unwearable. Then switching into a kind of general anaesthesia, our lucidity slipping, in a state of psychological fragility close to vertigo.

Back in my room, I tear off my clothes with the awkward urgency of an impetuous lover, the last ties I need to cut before I can sleep, and in the next moment I'm out cold in my XXL bed.

○ Ardabil is the capital of a province of the same name in the northern Azeri regions of Iran, at the foot of Mount Sabalan, an hour away on twisty roads from the shores of the Caspian Sea, a countryside that alternates between light grey and the intense green of fertile, arable lands. In winter, the snow erases the roads; the earth freezes.

I imagine Ardabil. Like other cities of this region, it is overshadowed by the domes of its historical monuments that stretch out from the Grand Bazaar, and is completely possessed by its taste for commerce, the buying and selling of fresh produce that spills out of the tiny stalls and collects at the customers' feet, smoked fish, gold charms, wood carvings and embroidered silks, pickled vegetables and pots of honey whose incomparable qualities are praised, in full-throated shouts, by men with moustaches and the physique of a skinny cat. I imagine Ardabil fixed in the timeless commerce that underpins its traditions, its way of life, and that is carried out below a series of sculpted, vaulted ceilings. Ardabil, where, since the dawn of time, cultures have met, currencies have changed hands, from one century to the next and back and forth across the Eurasian continent.

Based on some uncertain but convergent information, I have chosen early-twentieth-century Ardabil, which was doubtless such a town, as the place from which a boy by the name of Jacob Ghermezian, with only the shadow of his first moustache on his upper lip, set out, leading a donkey laden with rugs en route to Tehran. It was 1919. Jacob Ghermezian, the younger son of an impoverished Jewish family, was seventeen years old as he headed off on his first big journey.

I'm sticking my neck out, I'm making things up, because our digital archives say nothing about this exile or about what might have motivated the young man; and since his descendants are not generous with information and provide contradictory stories, I am resorting to guesswork. What did it mean to grow up in Ardabil or Tabriz or Maragheh in this part of the Caucasus that is now part of Iranian Azerbaijan and was much disputed by imperial Russia, outgoing Persia, the Ottoman Empire, and then the Soviets? What was it like to grow up at this crossroads of power and revolution, which probably did not have much to offer for a good economic future? All the more so because Jacob Ghermezian was Jewish.

And so he left, to find his subsistence elsewhere, selling rugs off the back of a donkey. And whether Tehran was his first stop or just where he ended up after a longer journey is such a minor point in regard to what followed that I am not going to bother with it.

Jacob Ghermezian devoted the rest of his life, which lasted almost a century, to getting rich. And this ceaseless pursuit, this flight forward, is what caused him to consciously or unconsciously reproduce the Grand Bazaar, where he earned his first tomans, and, decades later, many seas and an ocean away, in the distant and lonely west of this new continent, construct two of the largest megamalls of the planet: West Edmonton Mall and Mall of America. To his numerous descendants he passed on a financial empire worth more than two billion dollars as well as the notorious taste for business born of necessity.

◌ Jacob Ghermezian was already a prosperous rug merchant who had made his fortune in Tehran when he decided to immigrate to the United States in the late 1940s. He would have travelled with his wife, Miriam, and sons, Eskandar, Nader, Raphael, and Bahman, along with his fortune and other material possessions, by train or perhaps by road to Bandar Shahpur at the northern end of the Persian Gulf or to Bandar Abbas on the Strait of Hormuz, who knows? From there they would have continued by boat, around the Arabian Peninsula, through the Gulf of Aden, Bab el-Mandeb, the Red Sea, the Gulf of Suez, then on through the north–south canal by convoy, with pauses in the Great Bitter Lake, Port Said, the Mediterranean Sea, with rests here and there, then on past Gibraltar and its opening onto the endless Atlantic Ocean before disembarking, their skin salty from the winds and their inner ears in an uproar, at the foot of the Statue of Liberty, which lights up the world, and where fortune smiles on the most entrepreneurial.

Once in New York, Jacob Ghermezian imports and sells Persian rugs while his sons head to university, the eldest, Eskandar, to Montreal, from where he contributes to the development of the family business. By 1964 the Ghermezians own sixteen rug stores across North America, and the following year they start with land speculation, buying and reselling properties in the Ottawa area. During the economic boom of the early 1970s, Jacob establishes himself in Edmonton with Eskandar in order to further develop their business. With their money invested on the profitable side of the oil shock, the Ghermezians' funds multiply beyond expectations. The entire family ends up settling in the capital of Alberta, and a few years later they have become the largest owner of private property in the province.

In 1980, the recession that will last a decade is just starting when Jacob Ghermezian, an alert octogenarian, is struck by a genius counter-cyclical idea. Perhaps recalling the Grand Bazaar of Ardabil or Tabriz or Tehran, he decides to invest in the consumer sector. A project worth 200 million dollars that local pundits unanimously label suicidal, West Edmonton Mall opens its doors in July 1981, with 220 stores on a surface of 106,000 square metres.

And despite the fact that everything, from the geographic location to the economic context, spells failure for this oversized shopping centre, its successful audacity gives the man henceforth referred to as "Papa" Ghermezian an enormous lift.

Two years later he decides to double the reach and the size of his mall. No one among the locals, whom you have to picture as enormous North Americans, the sons and grandsons of lumberjacks, cattle ranchers, and gold miners, culturally inclined to believe only in wealth that comes from the earth itself—no one suggests that the little Jewish man from Iran should perhaps be locked up somewhere. "Phase II" of West Edmonton Mall adds no fewer than 240 stores, a skating rink, and the Bourbon Street replica to the already oversized complex.

In 1986, Alberta's recession is in full swing. The Ghermezians, still in the throes of their counter-cyclical faith overlaid with hubris, add another 280,000 square metres to their shopping centre, which enthrones it at the very top of the list of the world's biggest malls. This time the extension provides evidence of how much "Papa" and his sons admire the Las Vegas model. It includes a giant waterpark, a mini-golf course, the Fantasyland Hotel, and an artificial lake, dubbed Deep Sea Adventure Lake, with dolphins, a submarine, and the reproduction of the *Santa Maria*. (Since then the submarine has been removed because it required too much upkeep to be profitable, and animal rights groups have seen to it that the dolphins, who were very unhappy there, have been replaced by sea lions, who are probably no less unhappy.)

Construction is only just finished when the mall becomes the biggest tourist attraction in the province, a status it maintains to this day. By the year 2000, at the peak of its popularity, it is attracting 60 million visitors a year. The numbers have dropped by half since then, but the number of visitors to West Edmonton Mall still far outstrips those who visit the neighbouring national parks.

Jacob Ghermezian died at age ninety-eight, at the beginning of the new millennium and with his life's work at its zenith. His portrait hangs majestically in the boardroom of Triple Five, the diversified conglomerate that oversees the family's investments, and must naturally reduce the importance of whoever happens to be presiding at that board table. The picture is of a man wearing a black tie and a Borsalino hat, posed in front of an ornate bookcase, his mouth in a horizontal line and his left eyebrow raised in challenge. Almost at the centre of the photograph and against the black tailored suit, the light flashes on a medal awarded him by the government, recognizing a significant contribution to the well-being of his fellow citizens, to the community, and to all of Canada.

○ Thursday morning, seven o'clock, it's still dark outside. I've managed to sleep in two-hour bouts, broken up by partial viewing of low-end National Geographic documentaries—one on the discovery of the tomb of Tutankhamun and the other on the mysterious disappearance of an aircraft carrier in the Bermuda Triangle. I'm exhausted, suffering from insomnia, and everything except the thick duvet protecting me seems hostile, first and foremost the idea of a North American breakfast served on a tray in the food court of a shopping centre. I hunch over the screen of my cellphone in an attempt to forget my inadequacies, escape from this reality and the ridiculous idea of this trip. Rolled up in a ball, and with a rectangle of white light in hand, I check the news from home.

Photos and sweet words show me a father and son who are reinventing their routine, without the awkward mother that I am. I miss them. My son, like a ghostly part of my body, a part that has been amputated and whose signals my brain is still seeking. And P., like an alternative body, this body that isn't mine, and that somehow is also mine, and which I love beyond what he is or I am, a satellite body, a magnet body that extends me and makes everything possible.

I miss them, but they are doing fine without me. And I am doing fine without them. We have become optional for each other. I could disappear for a long time, maybe forever. That is an idea I find very comforting.

○ I have a meeting with M.D., vice president of Edmonton Tourism, whose offices are downtown. This is my chance to check, as I walk through it, that downtown is indeed clinically dead. Jacob Ghermezian and his mall have literally sucked the population westward. But the city doesn't bear a grudge. "West Edmonton Mall has brought us a lot," says M.D. "First of all, from the point of view of promotion: Edmonton is a small city, but wherever you go, including Europe, people have heard of it. And that is thanks to the mall! We can say that he's the one who put us on the world map."

Even more so because of the world records. If a certain building is the biggest, the highest, the quantitatively most spectacular in its class, it is sure to be a celebrity, its story told on media channels that are more and more competitive, the Top 10 and other superlatives. Which is why West Edmonton Mall, the largest on earth for quite some time but overtaken within a decade of its completion by Asian gigantism and Middle Eastern megalomania, continues to list the absurd records it still holds in its promotional materials: WEM has the biggest indoor roller coaster with a triple loop. It also has the biggest wave pool in the universe and the planet's biggest artificial lake with a roof. Soon it will host the biggest phosphorescent mini-golf course ever designed in our galaxy. WEM is like an aging celebrity who knows they are obsolete but who keeps muttering on about the vestiges of their glory.

M.D., who is British, around fifty years old, and wearing glasses, came to the great prairies of Alberta twenty years earlier, for love. She has recently moved from her distant village to the city, for reasons she doesn't divulge, and taken a job in the office for economic and tourism development.

Her experience of small-town Canada goes some way to explaining the ongoing success of the Ghermezians' mall. "Our population is spread over an immense territory. When people go shopping, they want to be able to buy everything they need in one place. WEM attracts customers from 500 kilometres away, and that's just for ordinary shopping. I know one family that lives about nine hours away from here and every year books two nights in the Fantasyland Hotel in order to buy school supplies before school starts back in September. They also visit the waterpark, where the temperature is 30 degrees all year round, see the latest movies, take in the restaurants, and window-shop for the latest fashions."

The four-star Fantasyland Hotel has 355 rooms and is located in the mall. Its décor is that of an amusement park, and you can spend the night with your family in an African room with a leopard-print carpet, an igloo room with papier-mâché snowdrifts on the ceiling, or a Polynesian room with palm trees.

M.D. says the mall's commercial offerings are as complete as that of any city centre in the world, and its climatic conditions are absolutely stable. She tells me that brands wishing to test the Canadian market often choose West Edmonton Mall for their first store. Some even set up their flagship store there; for instance—and I'm quoting her—the American lingerie giant Victoria's Secret, which has its biggest Canadian store at the mall.

Because of its dynamic management model, the mall always has something new to offer, says M.D. "A big Tiffany jewellery store opened up just before Christmas and had a huge influx of customers! Go, take a look. It's really impressive. That kind of success is evidence of the exceptional economic growth of this region."

M.D. is not the official spokesperson for the mall. She promotes tourism for the city of Edmonton. But these two functions actually converge. By moving the city's centre of gravity to their mall, the

Ghermezians have ended up privatizing the very idea of a capital, a big city, a city and its marketplace, where you also go for news, like in the Middle Ages. In fact, the centre of a city is by definition the commercial centre. And whether this centre is historic or prefabricated, the biggest and most popular one wins. In its ambition and its gigantic scale, West Edmonton Mall has absorbed public space and digested it as retailtainment.

○ Two days at West Edmonton Mall, two days that could be reduced to nothing or dissolve in eternity. Time doesn't pass the same way in a big shopping centre, and even less so with jet lag. The sun never sets in the country of commerce; if it did, it might make it easier for me to adapt. In my experience, a body that crosses eight time zones and is then deprived of the rhythms of astronomy has no ground underfoot and weighs heavy. Worse, when there are no temporal waymarks, the disappearance of geographical ones compounds the problem. When nothing is different—not the air temperature or the customs or the spaces—the body does not have to adapt. Left to itself, it slides along, with no obstacles in its path, in an unquiet kind of freedom that can become an ordeal.

In the mall's main thoroughfare, the fast-fashion shops follow one after the other, and all look alike, selling the same clothing—made in Bangladesh—but under different brand names. They alternate with smaller stores that sell shoes or handbags or sports clothing, perfume, eyeglasses, or cellphones, all international brands.

The manager of WEM tells me that the rules of commercial real estate apply here as they do everywhere else, and the rent per square metre depends on how much exposure you have to the flow of shoppers.

In fact, the shopping centre itself sets up the hierarchy: the central thoroughfares, well-lit and interspersed with fountains, rest areas, and refreshment stands, are zones with heavy traffic and high rents that host global brands and luxury shops, the only ones that can afford to invest and turn a profit. And so, the most visible spaces are inevitably reserved for goods and services that are all alike, cater to compulsive shopping, have to do with self-image and the inessential.

This relegates alternative worlds, weird or unusual interests, and stores for the aged or oversized, all those that cannot afford a space in the main shopping lanes, to the periphery. To access goods and services that fill an occasional need, or interests that are deliberately or unwittingly marginal, you have to walk much farther and venture into the least attractive areas. This is where I encounter a few shops for plus-sized women, a comic book store whose salesperson has a Wolverine haircut, an army surplus store that also sells guns, a lot of spa-nail salons accessible with or without appointment, an all-in-one hairdresser-tattoo-piercing place, a bookstore, a pet shop, an ophthalmologist, an ecumenical chapel, a continuing education centre, a post office, a shoemaker, an aqua-massage place, and a minuscule stall full of jade amulets, fossils, and the horns of triceratops.

☼ I step into this amazing place. It is run by a small man of Lebanese origin, about sixty years old, who introduces himself as a doctor of geology. I tell him who I am and why I'm there. "You're in the right spot! Just this morning when I opened up I thought about what a blessing this mall is for us all. I really don't know what this city would be like without it," exclaims Doctor G.

In 1986, when Jacob Ghermezian expanded his mall for the third time, he was looking for new tenants and was not particularly choosy. It was more important to ensure the rental income than the quality of the merchandise. Doctor G. had had a gem store downtown for three years, and Edmonton was engulfed in an economic downturn. Moving to what became the city's sole high-traffic shopping area saved him from being abandoned and bankrupt.

Doctor G. sells all kinds of stones, some already worked into gems, some still in their original form, as well as a huge collection of fossils he has dug up himself. "This *Paradoxides* trilobite, for instance, took me twelve months of work." Parting with these treasures is both necessary and painful. And some of the objects he has for sale would be more appropriately placed in a museum. Like the triceratops horn.

Oddly located right next to a dental clinic in a rather dead part of the mall, where the biggest attraction is a casino called Caesar's Bingo, Doctor G. receives scientists from the whole region who come to consult him on their finds and ask for advice. "There's a huge added intellectual value," he says. "And in some ways, shops like mine increase the prestige of a shopping centre," he adds with conviction.

I leave the four square metres of Doctor G.'s shop, but not before benefiting from a master class on the comparative qualities of local minerals and the work involved in cleaning fossilized Cretaceous fish. As a gift, I receive a small ammolite that is typical of Albertan subsoils, which should bring me luck if I always keep it on me.

Back on the main thoroughfare, I wonder what our malls or even our city centres would look like if nothing or no one decided in advance what might serve for impulse buying and what constitutes a wild extravagance. With time on your hands, you might then be able to step into Doctor G.'s shop, located on the main square, instead of testing out perfumes or trying on sunglasses. You might then spend 299 Canadian dollars on a Cretaceous trilobite and not on that fourth pair of sunglasses, which, like all the others, will fail to give meaning to your life.

◌ How can you spend a whole day in a shopping centre? How can you spend twenty-three days there?

I meet L. at the edge of the small illuminated fountain that decorates the busiest artery of West Edmonton Mall. A few round black leather poufs offer you an unforgettable view of a shiny yellow convertible parked on the plexiglass bridge above the fountain. This car is being offered as the grand prize in a contest, the kind that is run in malls on six continents, and for which you simply submit three random receipts to participate in a lucky draw. (What is this strange alliance between shopping centres and car manufacturers that triggers the same kind of contest all over the world and starts from the assumption that a gaudy convertible is the most desirable gift ever?)

L. is sitting on one of the poufs, focused on her cellphone, while two small children play close by with a stroller shaped like a car, observed with the same inattention by another, less attractive, woman. L. is wearing a short, belted Canada Goose parka, open over her deep décolleté. It is fluorescent orange, and its fur-trimmed hood makes her look very broad shouldered. L. has the build of a mouse, and the silicone breasts attached to this frame are too big for her. With her face covered in a thick layer of makeup and enhanced by four layers of spectacular fake eyelashes, she looks like a blow-up doll.

I don't know if she knows how bored she is, and even after she's told me her life story, I'm not sure. Either this woman knows her existence is futile and is desperately trying to forget this, or she's not aware because she's never known any kind of fulfillment. Here is the life of L., as told to me in a quiet monotone.

Every day, that is at least 360 times a year, L. comes to West Edmonton Mall. Most of the time she comes alone, sometimes with a girlfriend. During school holidays she brings her two boys, aged four and seven, the two kids playing with the stroller-car under the eyes of their nanny. She spends between 300 and 1,500 Canadian dollars a day. I calculate that this makes an average of 27,000 Canadian dollars a month, and controlling an impulse to widen my eyes I ask whether, on occasion, her husband has time to come with her. She says no, he works a lot, he's not always around, but she doesn't know exactly what he does. Something to do with oil, a job she knows absolutely nothing about, a fact she doesn't hide. Family holidays are rare. And so is time spent as a couple.

Every day at West Edmonton Mall she goes to different shops, but she likes the ones on the first floor, the upscale stores, best. She hasn't bought much today. Just some underwear from La Senza and two perfumes from Sephora.

L. talks to me as though she weren't talking to me. She doesn't ask why I'm asking questions. My interest in her doesn't make her happy. Or anxious. Given the reflections in her dark eyes, I wonder if she's floating in a cloud of barbiturates.

How can you spend an entire day in a shopping centre? How can you spend twenty-three days there? With a solid daily cocktail of tranquilizers, splashed with alcohol and flambéed with soft drugs, it may well be possible to spend an entire lifetime there.

☼ Rested and in a good mood, the cyclothymia of travel. This morning is no longer just the day after yesterday. The world is opening up to me; it is temperate, air-conditioned, easy to live in. All I have to do is cross the street and more than 800 stores offer to fulfill all my basic needs—food, entertainment, self-confidence— in exchange for money. I wonder if after my meal I should go for a swim, or visit the aquarium and the sea lions, or go to the movies. The beach is two minutes away from the multiplex. I wonder if I should reinvent myself. Buy a new suitcase and fill it with a new personality.

And what if I grew to love shopping? And disconnected my brain, let myself wallow in experiential leisure-shopping? All I would need to do is clamber over the mental blocks that prevent me from just enjoying and vanish into humdrum hedonism. So little, almost nothing, separates me from the debt-ridden middle class.

☼ J.S. is the executive VP of West Edmonton Mall. Big gestures, deluxe aftershave, in his late thirties, baldness pending, medium height, athletic body, cufflinks, a five-figure monthly salary. We meet in the Triple Five boardroom, where he takes a seat at the head of the table in the director's chair, his legs spread wide to let me know he's got big ones. Above him looms the photo of "Papa" Ghermezian.

J.S. is not a member of the family. But he's been in the family business for seventeen years, virtually bottle-fed on the Jewish Iranian work ethic. Because I am an unimportant interviewer, and doubtless because I am a woman and, even worse, using a foreign language, J.S. feels the instinctive need to crush me. He talks quickly, well, and without stopping. He often leans his upper body into the reclining chair back and folds his fingers over his chest. When he moves, it is with full force. He takes up the space. Despite all his efforts, I know that J.S. will never be a caliph in the place of a Ghermezian. I know that he knows that too.

We talk about the state of shopping malls in North America, the economic conditions, the competition from online shopping, the megamall business model, operations management at WEM, security, and renovations currently under way.

I discover that these days a north-south divide runs along the 49th parallel and can affect the survival of a megamall. In the United States, the Mall of America was seriously hit by the economic crisis after 2008 and is still struggling to recover, while in Canada, West Edmonton Mall has benefited from oil money accelerating its comeback. Comparable in size and administration, the two megamalls don't have the same resources with which to face the structural crisis that is ravaging the sector: the rise of online shopping.

Given the permanent change in consumer behaviour, WEM and the MoA both have the advantage of also being big enter- tainment centres. As long as people come to watch movies, have a swim, spend an evening in a piano bar, take a turn on bumper cars, or play a round of blackjack at the casino, the malls can maintain the statistics on client numbers that attract new stores and guarantee rents. The fact that this flow of clients has less and less to do with the purchases they make in the stores is not the mall's immediate problem; after all, it owns only the walls. During a recession, tenants are asked to be discreet about any difficulties they may be facing in order not to lower the tone. (The owner of a boutique about to shut down told me he'd been prohibited from posting notices that said "closing sale." Instead, he had to offer "exceptional sales" and quietly let his best customers know he was taking early retirement.) Any space that becomes vacant because of "natural" closure is recast for entertainment or some kind of counter-cyclical consumption, or handed over to chains and franchises. In other words, entertainment for the masses serves to keep rents at a level that are no longer justifiable in terms of their revenues. Of course, J.S. does not present these facts quite so cynically; this is my personal interpretation.

After an hour of conversation, my host crushes my hand and accompanies me to the door leading out of the Triple Five offices. They overlook Europa Boulevard, the mall's third themed street, after Bourbon Street and Chinatown. Two-storey papier-mâché façades "inspired by Europe's most beautiful capitals" front the stores that supposedly represent the tastes of the Old Country (they are mainly British franchises).

As we take leave of each other, we are simultaneously in Paris, Venice, and London.

⟡ The hours go by, the day too. I lean on the railing of the ice rink, watching a lesson for a group of retirees. I think, broken tailbone. I'm in an American Apparel store, trying out a scarf I don't believe in. I'm at the table of a coffee shop that is not Starbucks. I'm in a cinema showing the most recent film by Martin Scorsese. I talk to a sales clerk at North Face—she is twenty-two, earns 13 Canadian dollars an hour; West Edmonton Mall is the biggest employer of students in town.

I watch a sea turtle swim. I eat a cheeseburger at Swiss Chalet (in North America, Swiss = cheese). I sit on the edge of the fountain and spend thirty minutes counting the number of women with a shopping bag from a lingerie store, Victoria's Secret or La Senza (both of which are part of the L Brands group). One out of seven shoppers. I talk to a tall teenager who has just bought a knife in the army surplus store; he plans to join the army next year. I spend a quarter of an hour in a casino watching a large woman play a slot machine. A security guard asks me to move on. I step into the ecumenical chapel and come out two hours later. The people from the association that runs it tell me people sometimes get married there. A few months ago they held a funeral service. That was a first.

○ Tomorrow I'll be leaving for another continent.

When I thought up this trip, my hypothesis was that each stage would provide a cookie-cutter piece for an overview of the state of the world.

If so, what does West Edmonton Mall represent? Enormous, wide-open, lonely spaces, a harsh climate, an abundance of natural resources, labour as a mechanism for social climbing (which seems to work here). A pioneer spirit, oil and money. Come from faraway lands, merchants of facile forgetting can share the terrain with those who sell camouflage and ostentation. With the help of intermediaries, speculators, and producers of added value, the factories of the world that make low-cost products can sell their wares here. People can play at wanting to be together, with their family, their friends, but also as a community and in the world. You can meet individuals, personalities caught in their singular histories, looking for some kind of intoxication. The cyclical nature of the economy is reflected here, as are paradigm shifts, industrial revolutions, the survival instinct, the need to manage decline and make small compromises. You understand the idea that merchants have of market demands and buyers have of necessities.

In Edmonton, Alberta, where I have spent only sixty-two hours, I tot up these ingredients. I note how they mix and possibly merge, taking on what you might call a North American shape at this precise moment in their economic history. In other parts of the world, in other shopping centres, these ingredients will be similar but show slight differences. The cocktail will have a different colour, but the soup will be the same.

Tomorrow I'll be leaving for another continent. Checking out another one of these clusters, another one of these scenes, and three days later another one, and another one, in order, perhaps, to show how they're part of a grid.

Tomorrow I'll be leaving for another continent. At 5 a.m. I'll take a bus to the airport.

Then a plane and another plane. The trip has only just started.

VANCOUVER

THE FRASER RIVER starts in the Rockies, in the heart of the
mountains that separate British Columbia from Alberta. Before
it empties into the north Pacific, it travels over 1,375 kilometres,
digs through a basalt plateau, floods the bottoms of canyons,
then tears through woodlands to finally spill into the Strait of
Georgia.

The Fraser River estuary is a rich ecosystem that, for a long
time, was the territory of the Musqueam First Nation. A group
that was considered peaceable but which, perhaps gripped by the
intuition that history was not boding well, offered Simon Fraser,
a fur trader, and the twenty hairy, smelly men who landed with
him in 1808, laden with paddles, canoes, and cannon powder, an
exceptionally fierce welcome. When the explorer, who had been
paid by the North West Company to find a navigable route west
of the Rockies, reached his goal, he was met with arrows and
hostility and had to turn back.

The 1,375-kilometre ribbon of water was named after the auda-
cious Scottish fur trader in 1813, and half a century later, gold
prospectors came and founded Vancouver without asking the
Musqueam people for their advice.

The Vancouver International Airport today takes up most of a
small island, Sea Island, which is located at the mouth of one of

the northern arms of the river. The airport's glass interiors, criss-crossed with escalators and huge carpeted or polished granite passages, are decorated with monumental Indigenous art, large pieces of sculpted red cedar, painted in bright colours, that I am tempted to call "totem poles" because, like most of the other travellers transiting here, I know nothing about the traditions of the First Peoples of North America.

What purpose could these big objects have served originally? Set up in an airport, what are they meant to signify? Is the massive deployment of this aesthetic supposed to make up, if only a little, for the irreversible destruction of a culture in the rush for gold? Or is it part of the national fiction, the kind that suffuses the communications issued by tourist offices?

Whatever the functions of these objects, whether in the past or as imagined by their sculptors and sponsors, they seem to have one sole purpose today: to serve as a backdrop, a setting in which the people who use the airport can take selfies as travellers.

I see a group of Chinese travellers doing just that, taking selfies in front of a totem pole. Farther along, the same group is taking selfies in front of a shop window displaying souvenirs that look Indigenous but were actually manufactured in the country the travellers come from, on the other side of the north Pacific. An irony of globalization and the mindless flow of goods and people. Clearly, I am the only one who finds this funny.

My neighbour on the flight is Chinese, like the 300 other people on this A330 that is full as an egg and reeks of something both familiar and unpleasant, the breath of Asia itself, a sharp odour of fermented rice and chilies, a repressed odour of the gullet. I know it well. I remember it in Korea, in the public transport system, twenty years ago. Nowadays it sometimes floats as a residue in rooms housing only old people. I can live with this odour; it is part of my childhood.

My neighbour is travelling with seven men who all look like him, late-forties escapees from Maoism, with round faces, narrow, angular eyes, skin where acne has left holes and the sun melanomas. During the flight, they sometimes yell at each other over the seat-backs. My neighbour is the only one in the group, if not the entire plane, who is not seated next to a Chinese person.

This man and I will spend a total of 695 minutes side by side, reduced to occupying nothing more than the space our bodies take up, with arms and legs folded, forced into this proximity, this silent, embarrassed intimacy that only a long-distance flight can create. For most of this time together, our exchanges are limited to body odours, our basic needs, trips to the toilet.

Just before we arrive, and given the lack of privacy, I get the feeling that we are ripe for a conversation. I start one over the last meal.

○ My neighbour has been living in Ottawa for almost two years, an employee of the Chinese Embassy. The Air China 992 flight is the second of three connections that will take him back to Jiangjin, a small town located in a bend of the Yangtze River, in the urban agglomeration of Chongqing. (In the surrounding region, the rice paddies create pools of grey water and crescent-shaped terraces on the soft, intensely green sides of the hills.)

His work, which I gather has something to do with the upkeep of the embassy buildings, provides him with two months of vacation biennially (yes, every two years). Before Ottawa, he was in Washington for three years, which does not show up in his English proficiency—I have a hard time understanding him, and this is apparently mutual. I figure that in these five years he has spent four months with his family. The other 93.33 percent of his time has been shared with colleagues, exported Chinese manual labourers like him, probably in the space of a small apartment filled with bunkbeds.

My neighbour's life opens a window onto the condition of Chinese labourers, who seem to be rather numerous, and who are displaced in Asia and around the world in the service of their country and their more fortunate compatriots. I wonder whether, in the Chinese scale of inequalities, the fact that you share your daily life with your family, your spouse and child, as a nuclear family, isn't one of the greatest luxuries and, in fact, has the lowest priority when it comes to earning a living.

Somewhat later, just before we land, he asks what is bringing me to Beijing.

I should tell him I am writing a book on boredom. On repetition, on déjà vu, on replication, on the dysphasia of constructed landscapes, on the tackiness of the world and how it is shrinking, on the demise of the romantic journey, that European invention. I should tell him I am writing a book that examines how everything has become the same, undifferentiated uniform, dumbed down by what are called "best practices," the globalization of managers, those human resources that have all come out of the same mould with the same MBAs, with whom governments consult now and then for a mandate, for an audit, a benchmark, in case they want to build a mall or an airport. I should tell him I am writing a book on the fabrication of monotony in our cities and how it anaesthetizes all of us middle-class consumers around the world.

But, of course, I don't touch on any of this, on my distaste for the "system": I swallow my critique of the well-to-do, in the knowledge of how modern China is developing today, in cloned cities, and by what I glean of the Chinese condition from the eyes of my conversation partner.

For a moment I wonder what he has in his suitcases, what he is bringing home from Ottawa for his twelve-year-old daughter, his wife, his parents—kilos of consumer goods that doubtless come from some shopping mall, objects that reflect the North American dream and that will justify his absence for the short joyful time it takes to unpack them, before the silent embarrassment sets in—the silence of the daughter and her mother—in the face of this father, this husband, with whom they will spend the next two months, a stranger who isn't really one.

I tell him I am travelling on business. He smiles and asks no more questions, since that's what you expect on a flight to Beijing.

BEIJING

SEVEN YEARS AGO, seven light years given the development in Asia, I visited Beijing for the first time. The tourist experience at the time was largely un-subtitled, and the hostility toward strangers still palpable. What I remember is that Chinese was a language that yelled, except at Starbucks, those rare pockets of globalization that had reached the city. Unlike everywhere else, the baristas wore foundation makeup and murmured in the universal language that serves to order things like a "Grande Caramel Double Espresso Latte." That was before the Olympics. Since then, the central authorities have decreed that the country should be welcoming. The personnel at customs and in the hotels and restaurants has been replaced by people under twenty-five, who are personable and speak perfect English.

There are three of them, three young women, all made up, unwitting evidence of the successful starbuckization of China. An illuminated sign tells me the 186 "design" rooms of this high-rise with the glass-fronted ground floor are being managed by an American franchise, Aloft, which is one of the nine trademarks of the Starwood hotel consortium, a "middle- to high-class urban/ boutique hotel serving a young/business clientele."

I selected this hotel because you can sleep here for the equivalent of 49 euros a night and it is only a three-minute walk from the shopping centre I have come to see. I wonder if the other hotel guests have similar motivations. But what other guests, exactly?

From my room I can see the high-rise across the way, a Sheraton Four Points, one of the other Starwood trademarks. It has 355 rooms. Its façade shows nine lit-up windows. For several years now, Starwood has been pursuing a strategy of aggressive franchising that has allowed it to take over the very competitive but still unprofitable territory of China at a good price.

The Four Points and Aloft buildings were constructed in 2003, at the same time as a hundred others, all averaging twenty-five storeys, that bristle over this "Beijing Century City" neighbourhood, a sort of model city developed by the Chinese real estate group Golden Resources. It includes condos, offices, hotels, and, at its centre, a mall that for a brief moment was the largest in the world. The Golden Resources group is owned by Huang Rulun, an archetype of the self-made Chinese man, who holds one of the biggest fortunes in the country.

Golden Resources has built and continues to build model cities all around China. The group usually keeps a hand in the management of the entire real estate development and certain hotels. In Beijing, for instance, it manages the Beijing Century Hotel, an establishment with 554 rooms located a few hundred metres from the two hotels it has leased to Starwood. It also sublets certain spaces via long-term leases. A twenty-year lease for the mall, supposedly the beating heart of this prefabricated city, went to the Beijing New Yansha Commercial Company, a subsidiary of the Beijing Capital Retailing Group, which is part of the Beijing Capital Tourism Group, a creation of the Communist Party of China that trades on the stock market.

I do not understand the Chinese version of capitalism. And the seventy-two hours I spend there, right inside the materialist vector of this adopted economic system, simply deepen the chasm that hampers my understanding.

○ We meet in a Starbucks on the ground floor of the mall. Beijing is the only place where I treat myself to the services of a translator. Her name is P., she is thirty-one years old, friendly, efficient, and she seems to have the internet grafted onto her hand. Any question she can't answer in her head, she sends off to Baidu, the Chinese Google, her fingertips on her cellphone.

P. is interested in anything that isn't from here. But because she is self-employed, which is rare in her country, she cannot leave China. To get an exit visa, she would have to provide a certificate from an employer or prove she has a regular income. So she makes use of whatever her country imports: franchised coffee shops, movies on the web. A few years ago she had a Swedish boyfriend.

I ask P. if she ever goes to the shopping malls. "Never! I don't see why I would. Everything is cheaper on Taobao, and delivered to your home. Malls are pretty new in China. They've only been sprouting like mushrooms for the last ten or fifteen years. People aren't used to them, they keep using markets. And meanwhile Taobao has become really popular." All that to say, if the malls hadn't been built here, no one would miss them.

She's enthusiastic as she explains that Taobao allows anyone to sell anything they want, and that this has revolutionized commerce in her country. "It's like eBay. Anybody can set up an online business without a great investment. I buy everything on Taobao except food. And even that is changing."

Much like the 220 million Chinese who already use online shopping, P. sees malls as places where you waste your time and tire out your legs. Still, the Centre for Information on the Malls in China reckons that since 2000 their number has increased by 900 percent.

○ The *Mærsk Mc-Kinney Møller* is one of the biggest cargo vessels in the world. It is 400 metres long and 60 wide and can carry 18,270 twenty-foot containers. It comes first in the Triple E class, which comprises about twenty ships of this size.

With some imagination and pushing out the walls just a little, the Golden Resources New Yansha Mall, a parallelepiped rectangle that measures 575 metres by 100 metres over ten storeys, could contain two Triple Es side by side. When you know that these ships were designed for the Europe–Asia service, filled with virtually empty containers on the trip from west to east and laden with kilotons of all kinds of manufactured goods in the other direction, heading out of the ports of Qingdao, Shanghai, Ningbo, and Chiwan after the most efficient cranes in the world have done their work, then this reverse image can make your head spin.

The Golden Resources New Yansha Mall opened in 2004, claiming to offer the unsuspecting local population a "Western" shopping experience with "Chinese proportions." Its website lines up impressive figures: 550,000 square metres, 500 shops, more than 1,600 brands, 40 million goods, 50 different services, and 10,000 free parking spots for the 10 million or so visitors a year.

Two large department stores are located at each end, one of them managed by the New Yansha Commercial Company. Just like the rest of the building during my two-day visit, this place is completely devoid of clients. However, the number of personnel is spectacular. On each floor, an immense open space dedicated to a single type of product—accessories and cosmetics on the ground floor, women's fashions on the first floor, men's fashions on the second floor, etc.—is divided into squares measuring three metres by three metres. There are up to three saleswomen in each square. One to help you try things on, another to package the goods, and a third to run the cash.

About 10,000 people work in this mall, according to the management company. A typical saleswoman earns between 2,000 and 3,000 yuan a month (between 240 and 360 euros), which is the average price of a pair of shoes or a pot of French anti-wrinkle cream.

On the ground floor, and beyond the department store, is where you find the shops that sell gold or luxury gifts that

Chinese people exchange: swallows' nests, liqueurs made from roots, aphrodisiac sea cucumbers, and cartons of white-filter cigarettes. One large store, also on the ground floor, sells only high-end Chinese handicrafts, wooden sculptures and porcelain, whose sales are supported by another branch of the Beijing Capital Tourism Group.

Architecturally, the Golden Resources New Yansha Mall does not correspond to the American standards for this type of building. First, because there are too many floors, and second, because the ceilings are relatively low and there is hardly any natural light. Not to mention the illogical arrangement of the elevators and escalators.

As for what's on offer, the mall has not always looked the way it does today. You can still check the web for the items that were for sale the year it opened up. The stories describe a diverse and wacky assortment of stuff, but also tell of washrooms flooded by backed-up sewers. Basically, this was a place where the big European brands, dimmed by the Chinese mirage, were found next to the most unexpected shops—selling mouth harps or chicken feet. Ten years on, both the luxury brands and the odd Chinese shops have completely disappeared. The toilets are in better shape, but you can still come across a serious infestation of cockroaches.

The exact opposite of this early heterogeneity is now in place: only "upper middle class" and "family" brands are available, some Chinese but mainly international products that all represent the same image, hold up the same mirror: chic, relaxed sports clothing for men; elegant but not too exaggerated women's fashions, with an effect of uniformity that is enhanced by the way things are organized in zones and designated levels according to the segment of the public being addressed.

☉ P. and I stroll through this vast desert, and I wonder if all the people who aren't there are on Taobao. Traditionally, Mondays are dead for sales, at least in those parts of the world that have week-ends. Further, the development of online shopping has seen an increase in the phenomenon of what professionals in the business call showrooming: customers use the weekends to go to shopping centres, look, try on, touch the goods without buying anything. Back in the office on a Monday morning, they start their workweek with a discreet visit to the internet to compare prices and place orders. Monday is the best day of the week for Amazon. Showrooming is the reason client numbers in the malls are decreasing more slowly than their sales revenue.

The spokesperson for Golden Resources New Yansha, who can hardly be telling the truth, informs us that the mall has 50,000 to 80,000 visitors in the week, between 100,000 and 150,000 on weekends, and up to 200,000 on holidays. After spending a Monday and a Tuesday there, I humbly counter his statistics with a great feeling of emptiness and solitude.

○ In the afternoons, we sometimes come across women with a single child. Mothers, but mainly grandmothers. They sit on the edge of a big trampoline or a sandbox, at the foot of a climbing wall, or beside a gigantic pink plastic rabbit.

Families are the main target of the mall. One entire floor and half of the basement are dedicated to them. Thousands of square metres of toy stores, dozens of boutiques for pregnant women, play areas made of molded thermal plastic, clothing with international labels, huge quantities of childcare supplies, as well as classrooms for math and English from age two, and piano and karate studios. (In the karate studio an enormous, double-life-size, cardboard Bruce Lee cut-out stands next to one of Kung Fu Panda.)

In the shop windows and on the mall's flyers, pictures abound of smiling families in flowery gardens, all Caucasians, Papa in shirt sleeves, Mama wearing a dress, and two usually blond children, the older one a boy, who is sporty, and a girl, all soft and dressed in pink. The caption for these images could be "If you buy clothing from Baby Gap, and English courses at 3,500 yuan for five hours a week, your one Chinese child will end up being worth more than two Western children."

I ask P., who has no child for lack of time and money, what she thinks of the recent relaxing of the one-child policy. "It won't change anything, at least not in the cities. The priority for every-body these days is to make money. The women don't stop working if they have a child, not unless their husband is ultra-rich. In middle-class families, that means that the grandmother moves in and looks after the child. Wealthier people hire a nanny. In either case, you need to have the space. And you have to figure all the courses, the school books, the clothing, the stuff. Even when you have money, a child is a money pit. So having two…"

☼ The grounds around the high-rises in the neighbourhood are relatively green, or at least that is how it seems. It is winter, nothing is growing, but there are gardens, walkways through what is now dry lawn, and you can imagine that the bushes that are just black twigs could be in bloom. We encounter the same single chil-dren with mothers or grandmothers as we did in the mall.

Here's someone, running after a five-year-old. Madame X is forty-one. She is a stay-at-home mom, and of course appreciates all the efforts the mall puts out to please people like her. Twice a week she goes to the supermarket, taking her child along to play inside where the air is less polluted, she says. She has lived in the neighbourhood for seven years. At the time she and her husband bought their apartment, it was 5,000 yuan per square metre. Today it is worth eight times more.

When we talk to people, sometimes P., in a burst of curi-osity, asks spontaneous questions that turn into a conversation, completely excluding me. After a few sentences she ends up turning to me and explaining: Madame X has two children, and it's quite legal! Her older son is already sixteen. As a member of an ethnic minority, the Tujia from Chongqing region, she has a special status. And, P. concludes, "Her husband must be very rich."

○ We're back in the mall. P. doesn't say anything, but I sense her wondering what exactly I am doing there. It's a question I ask myself. If I were on my own, the absurdity of the situation would be less apparent.

Elsewhere, in Canada already, the indoor corridors that were lined with shop windows let me indulge in a kind of mental street-walking. I could think about everything and nothing, why commerce exists, the value of things, the nature of exoticism. The environment, bereft of quality, slipped over my retina, making room for reflection. I could enter my own head, because outside it there was nothing to see.

But with two of us, this is impossible. P. is my employee. I am paying her. I owe her some kind of direction, the certainty that we have a goal, which I am having trouble establishing for myself.

○ Two thousand eight hundred and fifty kilometres south of Beijing is Manila, the city that, along with Kuala Lumpur, has the greatest number of megamalls in the world.

It would not be unreasonable to trace the origins of this monstrous density to the 1898 Spanish–American War, which tipped the Philippines into the economic and cultural zones of American influence. But unlike the shopping centres east of the Pacific, which are slowly dying as the North American population migrates to the digital world, those in greater Manila are prospering as they offer local people a place for leisure and social contact well away from the humidity and heat, pollution, and organized crime.

The story of Huang Rulun, the real estate magnate who made the place where I am currently located rise from the ground, unfolded somewhere between the "mallified" capital city of these volcanic islands and the Golden Resources New Yansha Mall in Beijing.

Mental travelling. In the 1980s, the commercial neighbourhood of Binondo in Manila, around the small basilica of San Lorenzo Ruiz—a church in Hispano-colonial style that is dedicated to a Chinese-Filipino Catholic martyr—consisted of a network of alleys, flanked by two-storey apartment buildings with wooden slats, corrugated roofing, peeling paint, and windows covered in wire netting like bird cages, with laundry hung between two advertising panels for, say, Pepsi and Kodak film. At street level there were little shops for hardware, fried pork, textiles, their fronts protected by folding steel shutters.

Huang Rulun spent five years here, from 1986 to 1991, before he became the billionaire and philanthropist he is today, developing mysterious business activities in this part of Manila, which claims to be the oldest Chinatown in the world.

He started out with nothing, on the coastal region of the Taiwan Strait, where he left behind the peasant family that had not been able to send him to school. He spent the formative years that helped shape his entrepreneurial imagination in Manila. It was precisely in those years that the shores of Manila Bay were developed with megamalls, vertical city centres that are still among the largest in the world. The Sy family, of Chinese origin, which presided over the development of these mastodons, first made their fortune there, selling shoes.

Back in his native province of Fujian, Huang Rulun invested in commercial real estate in the early days of an economic boom that would make him rich. His vision of the ideal city, of which he has constructed various clones across China, always includes a shopping centre whose size is enormous and beyond discussion.

Huang Rulun has maintained an attachment to the Philippines that he doesn't conceal, especially as he has also maintained his business interests there. As one of the most generous philanthropists on the planet, he finances a drug treatment and rehabilitation centre about 100 kilometres north of Manila: a "mega-centre" of 10,000 beds, according to the Filipino press, set up in support of President Rodrigo Duterte's war on drugs.

The Philippines is home to about 700,000 people with an addiction to drugs. One fifth of the population lives below the poverty line. Ten million Filipinos have left their country in order to find better economic conditions for their lives.

One third of the thirty largest malls in the world are located in this archipelago.

○ P. and I pay some distracted attention to the prices of things. Whether it is textiles, shoes, or coffee, my translator tells me over and over again that the price of whatever it is has doubled since last year.

Statistically, P. belongs to the great middle class that is the dream of investors the world over. Her income is quite variable but, on the whole, she says she earns as much as her girlfriends who work in the service sector: about 7,000 yuan a month. She has just moved in with her boyfriend, who is a programmer; as an office worker, he too has now entered the category of the new IKEA customer. But because of rampant inflation, their household is having more and more difficulties paying its monthly bills, and has been reduced to buying only the essentials. If P. falls ill, she thinks long and hard before going to see a doctor.

She tells me there is a trendy new word for this emerging class in China to which she belongs: *yueguangzu.* It signifies "the people who spend their entire monthly salary." They earn good money, far more than earlier generations, but do not manage to save a penny.

But the *yueguangzu* are not only victims of inflation. Unlike their parents, they have to deal with a new kind of expense, which is tied to appearances. P. doesn't feel directly affected, but she tells me about her girlfriends: when a girl from the country finds work in an office in town, she wants to make a good impression, but she's not sure about fashion and her skin is rough. Fashion labels and luxury cosmetics serve as beacons, marking the way through the sea of consumer items for all those who come from nowhere.

○ A night is divided into segments, bouts of restless sleep, and television. The Paris correspondent of BBC World informs me that the president of France has a mistress. The rest of the news is about faraway assassinations and the polar vortex.

The ongoing voice of the news filters into my fatigue, covering and dissipating another small inner voice that is anxious and unclear.

As always in my dreams, I flee at the same time as I search. But I never find what I'm looking for; I don't even know what it is. My sleep is inhabited by a sense of silent urgency. The places I come through are always deceptive, more complicated than they seem, the walls hiding staircases that lead nowhere, elevators never stopping when you want them to, doors opening onto other stairs. They are labyrinths, often quite luminous, sometimes very lovely, which don't seem to be labyrinths because others are moving through them too, with graceful assurance. Caught up in my flight, and in my search, I see myself from a distance, nervous as a mouse in a balsa wood maze.

○ Mr. Z. gifts me a small wooden figurine in a glass cloche, a Caishen, the Taoist incarnation of financial prosperity, armed with a lance that can change iron to gold. In China, that is what people wish for most.

The scene plays out on the top floor of the mall in a drab, greenish-brown conference room whose walls show marks of water staining. A dozen worn vinyl chairs surround a long, wide table, which leaves little room to move around.

Mr. Z. is responsible for planning and marketing at Golden Resources New Yansha Mall. We have set up a meeting for a sham conversation; I had to submit my questions in advance, and he will now provide dull responses, as ready-made, wooden, and industrially produced as his Caishen.

During this conversation of the hearing impaired, P. does her work as an interpreter, but she can only deliver the basics, which is less than half of what I might grasp if Mr. Z. and I spoke the same language. Poise, accent, breadth of vocabulary, humour, repartee, all of which are clues to someone's background, their culture, their social origins, their professional competence, all of this eludes me, and in order to nourish my senses I am reduced to scrutinizing Mr. Z. and the fascinating details of his rather ugly round face. Because physically, Mr. Z. has nothing going for him.

As time goes on, his body slackens, his neck slowly subsides into the synthetic fabric of his epaulettes and almost disappears. His forearms, laid out flat on the table, end in a bouquet of yellow fingers with long dirty nails. The more he talks, the more I think about a clawed toad croaking away on a lily pad.

Mr. Z.'s discourse, as filtered through a double translation, from Chinese to English to French, as well as my own interpretation, provides me with the following: ten years ago, no one wanted to take on the management of a mall this size. The enormous dimensions and the concept of the building, built only to beat world records, were a real handicap.

At the time, there weren't enough Chinese brands to fill it. In the first years, 10 to 15 percent of the shops remained vacant. Since then, the company has refocused and is targeting a certain public. At the start the hope was to attract tourists as well as Beijing residents from a radius of about 300 kilometres, which turned out to be unrealistic. By concentrating on families and the neighbourhood residents, which already account for 2.24 million people, the mall now presents a clearer image and can better identify tenants. Today, all the shops are rented. The break-even point was reached within three years, which is remarkable according to international standards.

Mr. Z. states that the per capita profit earned by his company, which employs 150 people in the mall's administration, is among the best in the group (just to remind readers: Beijing Capital Retailing Group, a branch of Beijing Capital Tourism Group). The per capita or per employee profit seems to be one of the main ways to measure a state-owned company's earnings in China.

Mr. Z., who must be in his fifties, has been working for the Beijing New Yansha Commercial Company for nine years, ever since the mall opened. He says that he and his colleagues learned their business by travelling to see other megamalls, in the United States, in England, and also West Edmonton Mall in Alberta. And they contracted the services of international consultants.

He claims a number of key points contribute to the success of the mall, and he presents them via PowerPoint: lifestyle, the selection of food and drink, the play and rest areas, the entertainment options, the educational offerings, and finally, the shops themselves.

Mr. Z. says his mall still has three weak points: the entertainment infrastructure, because it doesn't yet have a roller coaster or bumper cars or a skating rink; the general ambience, because the décor and the rest areas are not attractive enough, with only the occasional bench punctuating the long hallways and only a few banners hanging over the escalators; and the selection of shops, which is not "exclusive" enough when compared to other malls. Mr. Z. aims to offer more original brands that are not available anywhere else in China—he calls this giving the mall a "personality."

When I see the way developing countries, in this case in Asia, seem to copy the worst aspects of the West (or the best ones, depending on your perspective), breaking the model down into set pieces they recite and put in place as though they were magic formulas, I am often torn between admiration and despair. Admiration, because these methods can bring immediate results that translate into cash growth rates. (A schematic explanation based on the Chinese mall: adopting the language of PowerPoint = greater international credibility = potential to attract new brands to China = rental income over three years, the term of a lease = increase in profits per capita = greater international credibility. In strictly financial terms, this is definitely a virtuous circle.) Despair, because these methods, which provide immediate financial satisfaction—but last only a limited amount of time, let's be realistic—also cause a kind of acculturation that has lasting effects. This oversized shopping centre, full of international brands and multiplex cinemas that reek of sugary popcorn, proposes behaviours and leisure activities whose origins no one knows and which deform the idea the local population may develop about modernity. For the children of the neighbourhood, the mall might be the only cultural horizon.

After thirty minutes of interview, Mr. Z. leaps from his chair like a startled bullfrog, claiming he needs to make an urgent phone call. He returns three minutes later with tobacco smoke on his breath.

Our meeting ends with a visit to the offices of the Beijing New Yansha Commercial Company. In Mr. Z.'s office, a few iridescent fish swim in an aquarium.

◌ P. is tired. For two days she has been listening and talking in two languages. For a change from Starbucks, we go to McCafé, the McDonald's coffee shop. I am thankful that she comes along. Our relationship exists for a fee, but this doesn't preclude feelings.

Because we're getting to the end of our time together, we digress from our topic and eat pastries, and for once, I am the one talking to her. About my life in Switzerland, my weak roots in Korea, and suddenly she brightens, finally understanding the origin of this look of two worlds I have in my face and that she hasn't dared ask about.

She says the Chinese adore what she calls "mixed blood" in English. Several big stars of Chinese pop culture are part

American, and their success supposedly derives from their big "natural" eyes—i.e., they haven't had plastic surgery.

She doesn't really believe me when I say that in Korea this mixed blood was long a synonym of shame. I don't know what it stands for today, but when I was born, this type of racial mixing, which was quite frequent because of the country's economic and military dependence on the West, almost always ended up with the children in orphanages or, in the best-case scenarios, with the exile of the errant parents. A lasting effect of the original dishonour that is inscribed in my face is that I can still find it difficult to look at myself in a mirror, where I see the traits of a father I don't know in the contours of a country that didn't want me.

P., who feels she is suffocating in China and dreams of everything that comes from elsewhere, says she envies me. She talks about her parents, her father a doctor in the military, her mother a businesswoman, who makes money the way only Chinese people can. A rich family, a well-established background on the edge of the state apparatus, which has given her the confidence to take risks. With a diploma in management, she devised this unusual profession, a hired assistant for journalists lost in China. I envy her solid roots while she sees them as chains.

We take leave of each other as friends. P.'s company over two days has cost me 2,600 yuan, the equivalent of 350 euros.

○ Mysterious China, the cliché that is regularly trotted out as the flavour of the week. Where the basic laws of supply and demand and good economic sense fade away before prophecies of imminent prosperity. The middle class shall emerge tomorrow.

In the early hours of the morning, not a star is shining on this surreal neighbourhood where 1,100 mid-range to expensive hotel rooms compete for a non-existent clientele of tourists, long-awaited at this enormous mall that is almost always empty.

I am not leaving a country; I am leaving a dream. The dream of a man, like so many others in China, who builds cities in line with his faith in the economic potential of his fellow citizens. They were too big yesterday, and they are too big today—the hotels, the malls, and the utopian cities will have to wait for tomorrow, quite indifferent to the skeptical gaze of people like me, who traverse the present in a dark mood.

○ My driver is wearing white gloves. It's a limo-taxi. The interior smells of roses. The highway is a racecourse at 100 kilometres an hour. The residential towers are standing in line, all looking alike from my place at the window, anthracite clusters, melting into the night. Sometimes, for a few seconds, the landscape flattens out. Sites for development, utopias under construction.

On the road again. Get out of the taxi, pay in yuan. Check in, wait. Cappuccino-croissant in a bistro done up like a trattoria. Wait some more. Security check, take out bottles and electronics, take off my boots, put them on again, repack my things. Take the train, change terminals. Daybreak. Spend an hour in a duty-free souvenir shop. Hesitate between this and that, think about those I love, a key ring for him, a jade pendant for her. A garland of animal shapes in padded silk. A mug decorated with a dragon. Stuffed pandas, imitation bamboo pens, local alcohol, mini-pots of Tiger Balm. Ashtrays, snow globes, neckties, sets of ten postcards.

I board and haven't bought a thing. At a certain cynical point, there are no souvenirs for anyone.

SINGAPORE

BEIJING TO KUALA LUMPUR, 4,500 kilometres due south, with a hook at the far southern end of the Malay Peninsula where
Changi Airport provides all connections to equatorial Asia. I am
flying with Singapore Airlines.

On the left side of a Boeing 777-200, I am sitting next to a
wealthy Chinese couple in their sixties. Madame, who is next to
me, is wearing very showy jewellery and a skin-tight outfit with
a glittery leopard motif. Monsieur, in the aisle seat, is travelling in a casually elegant suit that bears the discreet logo of a
major English brand. In a plane, you recognize frequent fliers by
the equipment they carry and the way they arrange it, system-
atic and confident in the confined space that is theirs. Madame
opens up a thirteen-inch tablet, a smartphone of the latest style,
earphones on white cables, a small bag full of ointments and
sprays. Wrapped around her neck, from before takeoff, is a satiny
tiger-print cushion. Her husband has the same electronic gear,
but unlike his wife, who has encased hers in protective covers
that can only be described as girly, he has selected dark leather
cases. He also has a small pile of newspapers and magazines in
English and Chinese.

A relatively well-off frequent flier can assert their individuality
with an array of portable screens that serve for entertainment, or

53

at least the possibility this represents to avoid the default offerings in the console on the seatback in front. It is a possibility that often remains virtual, or just ostentatious, because since too much choice negates choice, such a traveller will often end up like the others, watching some movie on the console, usually one of the new Hollywood productions promoted by the inflight magazine.

I remember the long-haul flights I took as a child, when everyone would watch the same thing at the same time on ridiculously small screens attached to the ceiling of the cabin. The best airlines would show the most recent movies, the ones that were just out in the cinemas, and it was a joy to read the program. Very often, from my perspective as a kid, that entertainment, regardless of how inappropriate it was for my taste and my age, was the icing on the already prestigious cake of being on an intercontinental flight.

As our electronic gadgets have grown smaller, commercial air travel has become more democratic, and I realize I have virtually no memory of the last long-haul flights I took. The inflight hours, reduced to an orgy of moving images, binge viewing, compulsive fascination with the worst of Hollywood, leave you with a vague feeling of shame at the time wasted in the search for oblivion, a feeling close to a hangover. Paris–Salt Lake City: was that the time I watched *Legally Blonde* 2, *Mission: Impossible* 4, and a couple of old episodes of *Friends*? Or am I confusing that with Frankfurt–Doha, where I took in *Iron Man*, a film with Jude Law and Kate Winslet whose title I've forgotten, *Braveheart*, *X-Men* 3, and *Chicken Run*?

The longer such a journey lasts, the more it becomes a chore that must be erased from your consciousness with some mindless filler—to such an extent that a transatlantic trip may disappear completely from your memory. Or, worse, be confused with a flight you took diagonally across the Balkans and the Middle East.

○ Layover in Singapore: a few hours in an airport I know well, where gardens of orchids and artificial ponds disrupt the blue-green carpeting.

Everywhere, at ticket counters, washrooms, the exits of stores or play areas, touchscreens are mounted on lecterns to let users express their satisfaction, with the help of five emoticons. These gadgets may well be used to index the salaries of the workers assigned to those services—though this is just an intuition—allowing management to periodically lower the pay or just let it stagnate, since, generally, only those who are not satisfied will take the time to express themselves, whether at the ballot box or on their way out of an airport washroom.

KUALA LUMPUR

THE MALAYSIA WE IMAGINE has something British about it,
luxuriant and colonial. It basks before a jungle background, with
rich biodiversity, and sticks to the skin like white linen below teak-
wood fan blades that churn the sweltering heat. The Malaysia we
imagine tells of pirates sailing across turquoise waters, heading up
muddy rivers, and three-mast ships arriving from northern Europe
to extract the fortunes and natural resources from the local kings,
who are plumed like toucans. It tells of feverish crew, deadly
mosquitoes, wreaths of orchids, and sweating skin, the derisible
import of ceremonial tea sets for use in the middle of mangrove
swamps, amid gigantic spiders and the reddish fur of proboscis
monkeys that run their long noses along the edge of the marquee.

Malaysia tells the history of a hyper-fertile land, swampy and
sensational, located along a navigable corridor; a peninsula
blessed for its location between India and China, and resembling
the pistil of a flower surrounded by the islands that are its petals.
Geological movements blew those islands out into the warm seas
so that boats could attach; they are shreds of jungle that tectonic
plates turned into a passageway for a procession of globalized
commerce.

Malaysia is a society of all sorts of faces, yellow, coppery, vari-
ously brown-toned, with slant eyes that are light or dark, round or

narrow, and a rare heterogeneous mix of religions and languages. As far as I can see, the merchants, the wealthy, and the prostitutes all come from China; the unskilled labour from the Indian subcontinent; the consultants from Britain. The contemporary history of the place is marked by the distinct status the Bumiputra people enjoy. The Bumiputra are the indigenous Muslim population—the original Malays, perhaps—people who, ever since the 1970s, have benefited from a law based on their supposed racial superiority, which gives them exclusive access to political power and administrative jobs.

This unique society, which is both diverse and racist, and where the Chinese hold 70 percent of the capital and the Malays 100 percent of the administrative power, has created an economic system in which corruption is an essential ingredient for the harmony that each segment of society displays, a wondrous harmony that is sold by tourist office brochures as a guarantee for a great holiday in the midst of a diverse population. The Malaysia of the postcards offers a sort of one-stop shop of ethnocultural stuff.

○ Ten hours and fifty-five minutes after I leave Beijing, I land in Kuala Lumpur in the mauve aura of the setting sun. Every pain in my body subsides in response to the tropical air. Nothing makes me happier than the hot, moist breath of a big Asian city.

In the orangey glow of the street lights, the city I cross by taxi unfolds in a vast disorder of concrete. Gutted skyscrapers everywhere, abandoned building sites, where at times the all-powerful vegetation that reigns in these parts has reasserted its rights. Some of it spreads onto the large traffic arteries, where it chokes an already difficult mobility.

As for the buildings that have reached completion, it is evident that developers can do whatever they want here, and usually in the megalomaniac proportions they prefer, without anyone counteracting with ideas about urban design or a vague set of development priorities, and even less with any concern for the aesthetic coherence of the neighbourhood—anything can, in fact, be resolved with a discreet financial arrangement. Money provides for utterly ridiculous construction projects in this country that is renowned for its corrupt administration.

It would be easy to hate Kuala Lumpur for all these reasons. But oblivious as I feel to ugly environments after several days of an absurd journey in a hard winter, I am ready to forgive the city everything from the moment it offers me its humid equatorial climate.

○ My hotel is a small thirty-storey tower right downtown. Forty metres across the way is one of the biggest and ugliest constructs of creation, Berjaya Times Square, 700,000 square metres of glass and ochre-coloured concrete, half of which houses a shopping centre consisting of fifteen floors, extended at either end by twin towers that are about 200 metres tall. Inside the more or less cubic space that serves as the base for this building, there is an amusement park with roller coasters for people to enjoy without ever seeing the light of day, more than a thousand different stores, and a parking garage in the south-east corner of the building that extends to every floor. Where it faces the street, the façade is a little more than 150 metres long and has swallowed up the sidewalk, covering it with a five-storey arcade that rests on twenty square pillars of pink concrete.

From my hotel window, I see that four lanes of high-speed traffic and an elevated monorail separate me from this scandalously oversized heap of trash. Of course, within minutes of dropping off my suitcase, I am already planning to tour the place. It is 9:30 in the evening and I have just spent sixteen hours travelling after literally going halfway around the world in a week. My body is howling with fatigue. But the idea of peeling off a thick layer of winter clothes and heading out to melt, barefoot and bare-shouldered, into the thick breath of Asia is worth any promises a hotel bed might hold.

◌ I barely have time to cross the highway via a pedestrian bridge lined with kiosks—plastic kitchen utensils here, fragrant soaps or sugary roasted almonds there—when Berjaya Times Square closes its doors. Inside, the metal shutters have already been pulled down and the last customers are leaving the complex, though a few people are wandering over to the multiplex cinema that operates until late into the night.

In my eagerness to visit the place, I had the night markets and nocturnal shopping centres of another Asia in mind, another time, other latitudes, where I could deal with my jet lag by going shopping at midnight, a pastime that is all the more pleasurable because it defies good sense (and the regulations that stipulate decent salaries).

But none of that applies here. At 10 p.m. all the doors are shut. I am a little disappointed.

◌ I am taking my time. The central lobby of the Berjaya Times Square, an enormous three-storey-high atrium, is richly decorated for the Chinese New Year: six large fake cherry trees in bloom have been set into the red carpeting. Huge scarlet lanterns inhabit the ceiling space like zeppelins in wartime skies.

Before leaving the atrium, people stop to take one last photo in this fairy-tale décor. A selfie in front of a cherry tree, a backlit selfie under a lantern, a group selfie with fingers in a V shape and a red curtain backdrop, a selfie on the way down the esca-lator, backward, to better capture the panorama. Those who like their photo stop dead in the middle of this fake orchard, their shoulders bent, their head focused on the cellphone, for the time it takes to post their production on some social media site, #BerjayaTimesSquare.

I watch a group engaged in a very elaborate and rather new sort of group selfie. Five young people are lined up in single file, their backs toward one of the cherry trees, their heads offset at random. The first one in line holds their screen vertically and at arm's length for an angled shot in which everyone has their place and can put on their most advantageous smile.

In all the malls in Kuala Lumpur, as well as those in Dubai and Casablanca, I observe such rites with some fascination, rituals that the vast majority of people submit to and that consist of taking a selfie in front of some spectacular object: brightly coloured décor, a dancing fountain, an indoor sculpture, a character built of papier mâché, someone in a teddy bear suit, under an upside-down bouquet of flowers, or in front of a modern art installation, since many of the managers of these shopping centres have decided to turn their establishments into galleries, even museums. And why not? Given the fact that the value has been lost to the function, a selfie in front of a sculpture by Jeff Koons is as worthwhile as one before a ballooning Shrek.

☼ I go out to embrace the urban chaos and humidity of the night that contrasts so sharply with the organized but downright ugly universe of the shopping centre. Outside, there are shadows, beggars, car horns, pollution, decrepit sidewalks, and storm sewers that can't soak up the rain. There's a smell of stagnant air, a vague feeling of danger, a hint of violence. Outside is this city that no one can master and that I wander through in my sandals, a light thrill of happiness in my spine and a knot in my stomach.

☼ I spend five days in Kuala Lumpur, four of them visiting eleven different shopping centres. On the fifth day, feverish with boredom, I flee into nature, to cleanse my head and my eyes far away from globalized commerce.

Kuala Lumpur is a mall-city. As far as I know there is not a single public space that is not enclosed and air-conditioned, with concrete slab or tile floors, electric lighting, and lined with shops. This may be a response to the equatorial climate. But it is also a response to the pathological increase in traffic, encouraged by the automotive and oil industries, which far exceeds the capacity of the existing infrastructure of roads and highways.

The shopping centres are the only pedestrian areas, replicas of dead-end streets whose outdoor aspect has become entirely optional. Without windows or natural light, these promenades could just as well be located underground. In order to escape the heat and the consequences of the economic, demographic, and urban growth that is constantly being promoted, people are

prepared to live like rats.

I have chosen to spend five days in Kuala Lumpur, less for its qualities as a mall-city—Singapore or Jakarta could have done the trick as well—than for the exceptional concentration of mega-malls that it offers (similar to Manila, it's true, but you have to make a choice). Three of the twenty biggest shopping centres of the world are located in this metropolis of 7.2 million residents, three megamalls that each boast between 320,000 and 465,000 square metres of commercial space.

The Petronas Towers, which were the world's highest skyscrapers from 1998 to 2004, loom over the cityscape, jutting into the sky like a pair of rockets, their mere presence justifying the ambitions of the country's real estate developers. At their feet, the city seems to roil in a tumult of cement in erection.

As I explore the actual city, it is yellow with pollution, red with congested traffic, suffocating in a vast selection of empty commercial spaces and unsold luxury apartments, delirious in its verticality, and riddled with construction sites, while in the distance, at the periphery, a housing crisis is under way, fuelled by the proliferation of those who are less wealthy.

There is obviously something irrational at work in this city, harking back to fevers, to the tropics and the jungle, to the proud debauchery of shapes and forms that living organisms can take on when they struggle for access to the light. Something crazy is emanating from this land and has become incarnate in the extravagant deployment of concrete that makes this metropolis monstrous, alienated, and fascinating.

◌ Ten malls, just a small sample, only a fraction of the commercial spaces that make up Kuala Lumpur, its flesh and bone. Two of them have received no more than half an hour of my attention, fatigue winning out over my professional conscience. What I remember is confused, piled up, or rather lined up, as though after entering the first of these malls I never found my way out. 1 Utama, Mid Valley Megamall, Sunway Pyramid, Berjaya Times Square, Suria KLCC, Plaza Low Yat, Sungei Wang Plaza, Lot 10, Fahrenheit88, Avenue K, kilometres of franchises, fast fashion, cosmetics, electronics, fast food, and coffee shops. A dizzying parade that is punctuated here and there, depending on the storey, with small shops selling Chinese knick-knacks or French luxury items; but the main body of the complex is always held together by the same businesses: Starbucks (in the most visible location as you enter the mall), Timberland, Bershka, Bata, Victoria's Secret, Michael Kors, Geox, Body Shop, Cotton On, Nike, Tumi, Adidas, Zara, Kipling, Gap, Beadbox, Puma, L'Occitane, Forever 21, Guess, Under Armour, Hush Puppies, New Balance, La Senza, Sunglass Hut, H&M, Levi's, Muji, Bobbi Brown, Topshop, Mothercare, Mango, Vans, Sephora, Swarovski, Clarks, Diesel, Uniqlo, Lacoste, Nars, Crocs, Banana Republic, Massimo Dutti, Yves Rocher, Samsung, Sony, Nokia, Lenovo, Toys "R" Us, Samsonite, Promod, Rip Curl, Tommy Hilfiger, Costa, Coffee Bean, Krispy Kreme, Dunkin' Donuts, Burger King, KFC, McDonald's, Pizza Hut, Subway, Häagen-Dazs; brands whose origins can hardly be traced anymore but that reassure the customer, signifying that the mall they grace with their presence is a world-class establishment, since the world in fact expresses itself via these labels, has been digested, simplified, and reconstituted in colour codes and slogans that present it as desirable, understandable, and ready-to-wear.

◌ I spend one morning in the company of P.S., a small man of Chinese origin who speaks English like a machine gun. He is the manager of 1 Utama, a complex of 465,000 square metres over six storeys, whose orange façade is faded from the exhaust fumes of the highway it overlooks. 1 Utama is the air-conditioned city centre of Bandar Utama, a gated neighbourhood of four square kilometres located at the periphery of Kuala Lumpur. It arose from the wasteland of a former palm grove in the early 1990s, along with its golf course, its clinic, and its private schools.

I have to wait till the end of our three-hour conversation for P.S. to finally admit that yes, perhaps the agglomeration of Kuala Lumpur is indeed suffering from an excess of commercial spaces. He takes me over to his office window. "See those construction sites over there? Next year, four new malls will be opening their doors on this highway. Big ones, little ones, it makes no difference. Four new malls. We have reached a point where this is starting to cause problems for our tenants, especially the big chains. Whenever a new shopping centre opens, those chains are almost forced to show up and occupy space. But as a result of having to be everywhere, and sometimes only a few hundred metres apart, they start cannibalizing each other. So they have to make a choice. And this makes negotiations more difficult for us. Unfortunately, nobody can stop the real estate developers. There are so many speculative projects in mixed-use neighbourhoods, and they all understand that shopping centres, necessarily..."

I don't know if the four new shopping malls planned in the 1 Utama neighbourhood count among the forty the association of real estate developers of Malaysia already has listed and which are expected to be in place in greater Kuala Lumpur by 2020. A dozen of them will measure 100,000 square metres or more.

"The Malaysian association of mall managers tries to see this development as positive and views the constant influx of new commercial spaces as an opportunity," P.S. tells me. "We are working to clearly position ourselves and differentiate ourselves from one another. We are also sending delegations abroad, to England, for instance, to South Korea, to Japan and Australia, to look for brands that might want to develop a franchise in Malaysia. Our country provides a good test case for southern Asia."

P.S. explains how the mall managers, who are all marketing a standard product—acres of tiled corridors lined with the same shops selling the same clothes, the same cinemas showing the same movies, the same amusement areas offering the same exciting experiences, the same skating rinks where the same population of young people and families moves round and round in the same direction in search of the same romanticized ideal of middle-class happiness, on the same prefab Sunday after-noons that all end up on the terrace of the same Starbucks—how these managers try to wrap all of this into words, images, loyalty programs, statistics, entertainment options, and façade resto-ration projects to make clients believe that mall A is different enough from mall B for it to be worthwhile for franchise X to open up a shop in each one. Because once both mall A and mall B offer the same commercial products, they will resemble each other even more, which will contribute to making the work of P.S. and his colleagues even more absurd.

To my mind, the Malaysian association of mall managers is like a conversation group for anonymous depressives, where people slap each other on the back and exchange falsified visitor statis-tics before bursting into belly laughs, a salute to despair.

○ Officially, Kuala Lumpur does not suffer from an excess of commercial space. On the contrary, it "benefits from this abun-dance," says N.Y., the director of the city's tourism office. An abundance that is not due to the municipal government giving in to the power of money, as one might wrongly assume, but to a cultural trait typical of the region: "In Malaysia, we like to shop."

N.Y. never had the time to meet with me to provide this infor-mation. In what may be another cultural trait of Malaysia, it is common to experience last-minute cancellations of meetings, avoidance of telephone calls, and a refusal to waste time responding to questions via email. Instead, questions from journalists are passed on to consultants, who receive lump sum payments to think on behalf of the authorities, and whose responses are sent out without further elaboration. Everything I received from N.Y. was first compiled on an electronic slide presentation by two employees of Roland Berger, a global management consulting company.

"This abundance of commercial space is a great marketing plus for Kuala Lumpur! CNN has classed us in fourth place among the best shopping cities in the world, and according to the Globe Shopper Index, we are second best in the Asia-Pacific region. Such recognition from international organizations positions us very advantageously on the world stage. The best tourist destinations of the world, such as Paris, London, and New York, all offer solid shopping options. Now Kuala Lumpur is on the way to becoming a first-class tourist destination, which presupposes matching shopping opportunities."

My summary: there is nothing to do in Kuala Lumpur except go shopping. All the best tourist destinations of the world provide great shopping opportunities, and so Kuala Lumpur is a great tourist destination.

○ V.C. began his professional career in the banking sector in Spain before moving on to the communication industry, where several positions in business development allowed him to strut his stuff—with an alpha male physique and well-aligned white teeth—across a number of emerging markets such as Bulgaria, Turkey, Russia, Lebanon, Algeria, Rwanda, Sierra Leone, Cameroon, and Malaysia, countries he has pinned to his CV like so many stamps in a collection.

Early in the new millennium, V.C. realized that a square jaw and a prominent brow might not suffice to truly launch his career; he needed an MBA (Master of Business Administration). And so he set out to buy one from INSEAD in Singapore (the French Institut européen d'administration des affaires), which has two schools abroad, the second located in Abu Dhabi. Armed with his diploma, he made his entry into the consulting business in 2004.

Today, V.C. is one of the supervisors in the offices of Roland Berger in Singapore. He thinks up investment strategies, international expansion strategies, and national industrial strategies; leads strategic projects in Southeast Asia, the Middle East, and Africa; and manages a portfolio of clients ranging from the public sector to real estate development, from tourism to telecommunications, from financial services to biotechnology.

Is V.C. superhuman? I am speculating, but it is obviously not the case. What he does to perfection is manipulate prefabricated models of thought that allow him to move about in any microeconomic system while seeming to adapt to it (the actual work of the consultant, in fact, consists of making those microeconomic systems he analyzes adapt to his own prefabricated thinking).

In his daily work, V.C. rereads and co-signs reports that have been put together by others like him, but who are at a lower hierarchical level—for instance, A.A., who has not yet acquired an MBA and runs the risk of seeing his career stagnate at the level of senior consultant if he does not obtain one.

A.A. holds a BA in chemistry from the University of Illinois. His first job after graduation was as an analyst for Capital One, an American company specializing in credit cards, automobile loans, and mortgages. That was in 2007, just before the entire world became aware of how companies such as Capital One had encouraged the poor of America to become over-indebted, and how this over-indebtedness, which was promoted and metabolized by the banking system, led to the world economy teetering on the brink of disaster.

A.A.'s first assignment involved "formulating strategies to improve the collection of interest owing, reduce credit risk, and improve operational efficiency." I am not making this up; that is actually what it says on his CV.

After successfully completing this first professional assignment, he was hired by Arthur D. Little, a consulting company, where he spent three years writing reports for the aviation industry, insurance companies, logistics firms, tech companies, and the public sector. Strategic and technical reports, long-term strategic planning, international development strategies, general management programs—A.A. could handle it all, including the cookie-cutter analyses that were part of his daily tool kit.

Once in Singapore, where he set out to enhance his professional competencies, A.A., like all the expats of his age and pedigree, who are legion in this city-state, learned how to drink large quantities of sugary cocktails from 6:30 p.m. onward without appearing too drunk by midnight, how to use social media to conceal the fact that he had forgotten the name of the person he spent the night with, how to be in the right WhatsApp groups that organize good *afterworks*, and how to distinguish the bars used by prostitutes from those for tourists.

◌ V.C. and A.A. are consultants with Roland Berger, to whom the municipality of Kuala Lumpur has delegated the task of drawing up its 2015–2025 General Plan for Tourism Development.

I picture A.A., his butt resting on a wheeled Vitra office chair with extendable backrest, his eyes fixed on a 40-inch LCD monitor as, a little hangover-slow, he uses a keyboard shortcut to open a new PowerPoint document in the Roland Berger colours. He inserts a spreadsheet on the second page of the PowerPoint and enters a series of column headings (in English) that provide a ready-made list of what a tourist supposedly expects: "Culture & Heritage," "Nature & Adventure," "Entertainment," "Food & Beverages," "Shopping," "Architecture." Isn't that exactly why we travel?

The second row of the first column lists the most interesting places in the city: the Petronas Towers, the national mosque, the aquarium in the Suria KLCC mall at the foot of the Petronas Towers, the Suria KLCC mall, Bukit Bintang (a neighbourhood that has the largest number of malls in the city), the amusement park in the Berjaya Times Square mall, and so on.

Where the rows and the columns intersect, small green check marks identify the existing features of Kuala Lumpur. The analysis is then completed with various other analytical diagrams, using SWOT, STEEPLE, or PEST methodologies, that don't provide much more information than is visible to the naked eye as you walk through the city centre.

The columns that are well-furnished with green check marks— "Shopping" and "Food & Drink," for example—are subjected to further treatment via short-term "valuations of existing assets," which V.C., dressed in a semi-bespoke suit, will then present to delegates of the municipality of Kuala Lumpur, assembled in an air-conditioned conference room. The delegation will have received the PowerPoint in advance, but no one will have read it.

For example, V.C. will say it would be opportune to produce some themed flyers for distribution at airports and tourist offices that propose itineraries, such as "Best of shopping," with beautiful images of sites to visit, some key statistics, one or two quotes, and a historical piece that lays out, say, the ethno-tribal origins of shopping on the Malay Peninsula.

The columns that are low on green check marks are exported to another slide presentation entitled "Long and medium-term development strategies," and accompanied with the same diagrams that reformulate good sense, risk aversion, and the absence of new ideas. They will translate into a long series of further meetings that will be led by V.C.'s system of bullet points. These meetings will most likely lead to a host of construction sites as low in ambition as they are high in optimism with regard to deadlines and budgets. Found to be weak in the column labelled "Nature & Adventure," Kuala Lumpur could thus see all sorts of "edutainment" complexes opening up by 2025, funded by petrodollars and

KUALA LUMPUR

underscored by a grade-school-level discourse on biodiversity—complexes that target middle-class families who will arrive there in their cars. The restaurants will be managed by the catering branch of some international restaurateur, and the souvenir shops will be subcontracted to the merchandising sector of the Disney group.

I hold these MBA-style methods of analysis, this way of thinking that consulting companies sell, directly responsible for the standardization of airports, shopping centres, museums, and tourist sites.

Moreover, this organized chain of delegating thought—the mayor of Kuala Lumpur delegates to N.Y., who delegates to V.C., who delegates to A.A., who uses standardized models to devise a tourism development strategy for what is today, but not for much longer, one of the most beautiful regions of the world—this succession of individuals systematically relinquishing their responsibilities is the reason for the implacable and systemic mechanism causing the uglification of the world.

○ For ten days now, over the course of the various different time zones, I have been waking up between two and four in the morning. While normally I sleep like a cat, anywhere and for a long time, I am discovering the horrors of not being able to rest even though my fatigue is increasing. Worse, the strange kind of insomnia I am suffering seems to be adapting to jet lag more quickly than I am: wherever I am it is 2 a.m. in my insomnia.

What do I do with this time I gain each night? I lose it in doubt, spend hours wandering in the forest of my anxieties. Some nights I put it to use, pragmatically, to prepare interviews, to write accounts of my trip; this topic that is too huge for me to even begin to describe. Sometimes, too, I use it to call home and catch up on news via video-conference, time difference allowing.

In KL I don't have Wi-Fi in my room, so I spend most of this time moping at the entrance of the hotel, away from the air conditioning, gazing into the limits of the flickering street lights in the silent company of a few taxi drivers.

My home is light years away. A time difference of several seasons separates me from my family. I get white-and-grey pictures, infused with winter; my little boy in a snowsuit. Here, I am bathing in jungle dampness. I now understand that my skin is the organ through which reality affects me the most. When I imagine those I love beside me, I dream of them seeing what I am seeing, experiencing what I have been experiencing during my trip, but these pictures from far away only emphasize their absence. They are feeling cold at the same time as I am hot. I have the physical feeling— transmitted from the pores of my skin to my brain—that I have abandoned those I love in a parallel time and space.

○ Malaysia is part of the zone of Chinese influence called the "bamboo network," which stretches across the whole of Southeast Asia. Deriving from the emigration of Chinese people at the most turbulent moments of their political history, the bamboo network has for the past century been spinning a web in which a parallel economy operates and moves money more freely than officially.

There is not a billionaire, not a single real estate speculator in this part of the world, whose life couldn't serve as an illustration of this system of personal interests structured around Confucian ethics and the loyalty this implies when family connections also involve financial interests. The bamboo network tells of lives that often resemble each other: a young man leaves a desolate part of the Chinese countryside and establishes himself in Indonesia or Taiwan or the Philippines or Malaysia, joining a brother-in-law, or a cousin, and slogs away like a madman, saving every penny of a very slim salary. After some time, the money he has amassed is invested in some business venture, selling natural resources or semi-manufactured products, a venture whose further development rests securely on a first generation of children entirely devoted to serving the family. A diversification phase follows at some point, usually in the direction of real estate, either in mainland China or in the expat location, in order to firmly settle the new fortune and grow it for years to come.

One example is the story of Teo Hang Sam: it starts with a famine and ends two generations later with the construction of a megamall. It bears some resemblance to the stories of Jacob Ghermezian and Huang Rulun, and I cannot help but wonder if somewhere behind these temples dedicated to abundance, behind this wish to found something large and perfectly ordered such as a city or the dream of a city centre, there might be some vaguely psychological explanation that derives from an early childhood experience of lack, something that might even apply by extension to consumer society as a whole. At the same time, I have to keep in mind the rags-to-riches story, a perfectly globalized genre of storytelling that can end up creating resemblances where in fact there is nothing but a carefully developed discourse.

And so, Teo Hang Sam left his hometown of Guangdong by ship in 1933 with several crates of mandarins on his back that he hoped to sell where he had heard he could get a better price. Soo Cheng, his second son, twelve years old, went with him. They were headed for the Malay Peninsula, 3,800 kilometres from the port of Shantou, where they boarded what must have been a junk. Given the speed of such boats, I estimate it took about twenty days to reach Port Klang.

At that time the Sultanate of Selangor offered business opportunities that the province of Canton, where people in the countryside were dying of starvation, did not. What started out as a return business trip turned into definitive exile when father and son were joined by the rest of the family: two other sons— the oldest, Soo Chuan, and the youngest, Soo Pin—as well as a number of daughters, which the family archives do not mention since in those times they simply didn't count.

In Kuala Lumpur, Teo Hang Sam began selling chicken and duck eggs at the central market, which his three sons delivered by bicycle.

Then he opened a small grocery store that did well during the Japanese occupation but was destroyed in the war. The day after that disaster, Soo Chuan and Soo Cheng left to look for work, since there were now ten mouths to feed in the family. They bought seven sacks of white sugar from a friend of their father, which they resold for more money on Petaling Street, the main street of Kuala Lumpur's Chinatown. That is how the story of See Hoy Chan, the Teo family's trading company, begins. See Hoy Chan could translate as "warehouse overflowing with goods from beyond the four seas." After the sugar, it was the trade in rice from Singapore to Thailand and Burma that made the family business its fortune and gave Teo Hang Sam the nickname "Rice King of Malaya."

In the late 1980s, Teo Soo Cheng built 1 Utama, which can literally be described as the "warehouse overflowing with goods from beyond the four seas" his father dreamed of. But I am not sure he actually made that connection. When he bought the four square kilometres of yellow soil that was once an old palm grove in the suburbs of Kuala Lumpur, Teo Soo Cheng was planning to develop one of those new townships, selling people who are eager to live as prisoners an exceptional quality of life that is modern, affordable, and in utter isolation—the "warehouse overflowing with goods from beyond the four seas" being merely a fragment of this greater utopia.

When I visited Bandar Utama and its mega-city-centre, Teo Soo Cheng appeared as withered as a small apple and as fragile as an old sparrow. He died a few months later in May 2014, at the age of ninety-three, and the entire community of Chinese businessmen in the Klang Valley rendered him emotional homage.

◌ On the sixth floor of a mall that is in full "strategic repositioning" mode, I find a small Kashmiri shop. It is wedged between the escalator and a series of construction site panels announcing the opening of "an exciting new experience." Selling jewellery and hand-embroidered textiles, the shop is surviving the construction work in remarkable isolation.

The owner is young, realistic, resilient, and business-minded. His shop provides income for a whole network of people between Kuala Lumpur, Singapore, and Srinagar. One of his brothers has also established himself in Malaysia, and together they run this store and a second one located in a hotel lobby, where, he tells me, business is much better.

We talk about tourism in KL. "Muslim tourists don't like to walk around," he says. "They just want to go directly from their hotel rooms to an escalator that will take them to the stores. The number of malls here, one right next to the other, is ideal for them. If they were linked by air-conditioned corridors it would be even better. Russians and older Americans are like that too. For KL, the bad tourists are the Europeans. You people like walking around outdoors all day long. Nobody here can understand that."

A study by DinarStandard (a consulting and strategic research company) projected that by 2020 the number of Muslim tourists would increase more rapidly than the average number of all the tourists in the world. The director of the plan for tourism development in Kuala Lumpur is very pleased: "With its Muslim-friendly atmosphere, accessible prayer rooms, and easy availability of halal food, KL is well positioned to attract these new tourists who are also high-spenders."

◌ In archival images, the black and white of history, I see Chinese women in long sleeves to protect against the sun, headscarves tied under their chins, wearing those large round pointy hats that we associate with work in the rice paddies. With their feet in the mud and leeches attached up to their knees, they are patiently washing river sand, swilling it round and round in large wooden bowls just below the surface of the water. The circular movements that engage their bodies from the shoulders to the lower back separate out the lighter particles of sand and send them into the water, leaving only the precious grains of tin in the bottom of the bowl, which, at the end of the day, the women take to a smelter where it is weighed, and they are paid.

They left Guangdong to go down the Klang Valley and seek their fortunes under the British flag. In the nineteenth century, Malaysia produced more than half the tin used in the world, and Chinese immigrants provided the manual labour to extract it.

Central Market, a building in colonial Art Deco style, is witness to this era. Built in 1888, then enlarged and renovated several times until 1937, this ancient covered market provided the Hakka exile community with the dietary complements for its basic sticky-rice diet: chickens and ducks, beef intestines, fish of the day, rubbery mushrooms, lettuce, and bitter melons.

Today, Central Market sells gaudy cellphone cases, keychains in the shape of the Petronas Towers, mugs that read *I Love Malaysia*, small leather goods, fairground candy, necklaces, plastic suitcases, souvenirs that cost less than 7 dollars, little wooden elephants, mini jewellery boxes, embroidered silk spectacle cases, wrought-iron business card holders, and all kinds of sarongs and shawls. All of these objects have been imported in shipping containers from poorly industrialized China.

Guangdong is now one of the richest areas of Asia.

◌ At the far end of a corridor that runs past rows of shops that all look alike, there's a mini-boutique of antique twentieth-century wares that seems to have been forgotten in the mallification process of Central Market. Inside, a small Chinese man in a straw hat is playing ukulele and singing like a Hawaiian crooner. All around him are piles of colourful objects that resemble him: assorted ceramics, plastic novelties, 33-rpm records of love songs, varnished metal and wood objects that speak of the colonial past, oxidized jewellery that, like everything else here, looks fake but is genuine, displayed behind glass where dust accumulates.

Mr. Y. is playing for one of his customers, a man of Indian origin, very tall, very elegant, dressed all in white linen, who appreciates the music but won't buy the set of turquoise British dishes bearing the Queen's portrait. The swarthy giant leaves empty-handed, but as a regular, perhaps a pensioner, certainly someone with free time, he will be back in a week.

Mr. Y.'s shop is a Gallic village, his very own rampart against the impoverishment of commerce (like Marguerite Duras's *Sea Wall*, a barrier against the Pacific). It serves as a meeting place for all those who are tired of disposable modernity: people with aesthetic interests, artists, passive resistors, who are even fewer than a minority in these latitudes. I meet a Chinese poet who earns his living by selling fried food, an older Australian architect who has seen it all, and a professor of painting from the School of Fine Arts, who regales me with long discourses on the megalomanic habits of rich Asians and the racial inequities that are plaguing his country.

Central Market is not the same as it was twenty years ago, when Mr. Y. established himself. In 1970 it was saved from demolition by a citizens' initiative that saw it labelled a historical monument, and it reopened in 1985 as an art and local handicrafts market. The bastion it was meant to represent against real estate speculation and its collateral damage did not last long.

In 2004 the Kha Seng Group, which specializes in the textile business, bought the building in a first step to diversify and move out of the sector. Three years later, probably not knowing what else to do with its money or capacity for credit, Kha Seng kicked off an enormous project a few kilometres away, building a twenty-two-storey high-rise, nine storeys of which became a shopping centre with 800 boutiques, all of them dealing in textiles. Shortly after that, the group bought a dead mall, also on the edge of the city, which had already gone bankrupt twice, and set out to turn it into a commercial centre for home furnishings and décor. As real estate developer and mall manager, the Kha Seng Group mobilized the famous synergies that have led to the flattening of commercial offerings across all its properties. Which is why Mr. Y. saw his old neighbours, gallery owners and artisans, some of whom were friends, systematically disappear to make room for vendors of cellphones and handbags.

Mr. Y. was born in the Klang Valley on the day of Elizabeth II's coronation. To celebrate this random moment that links him to the Crown of England, his shop collects all sorts of objects from across the Empire commemorating this date. The first job he held was as a policeman (he shows me a photo of himself as a young man thrusting out his uniformed chest), but, he says, he couldn't accept the highly corrupt practices of this powerful corporation. So he moved to Australia, studied theology, and became a pastor. Back in Kuala Lumpur, he preached for a while but then got fed up with a church that expected him to perform as a clown rather than deliver sermons, which he felt was an indignity. Mr. Y. is an honest man, happily cynical, lively and authentic, disappointed by a world he hides from at the far end of a mall—in other words, in his heart—behind a wall of old objects that speak for him and are hardly meant to be sold.

◌ There must be some relationship between the size of buildings and the profit margins of the economy in which they grow. This is what I tell myself as I walk through the park that surrounds the Petronas Towers.

Palm oil and rock oil, the lubricants of the Malaysian economy, position the country well ahead of product chains like Nutella, or cookies and ice cream. Well ahead also of the factories producing the plastic packages they are wrapped in, and the transportation systems that bring them to the sales outlets.

A pensioner economy. I think of Russia constructing a row of the tallest skyscrapers and the biggest malls in Europe. I think of the Arabian Peninsula, where Burj Khalifa, currently the tallest building in the world, marks the spot for kilometres of desert flatness around it, with the world's biggest shopping centre located at its feet. I think of the United States, which invented oil drilling, malls, and skyscrapers before anyone else.

The notable exception is China, which has some oil resources and is not really a pensioner economy except in its demographics: it seems that the highest buildings in the world are often located close to stocks of oil and gas.

I follow the contours of an artificial lake that extends the reflections of the Petronas Towers, a pond computer-designed to create nature in town, whose shores lead steadily and firmly straight to the entrance of a shopping centre (Suria KLCC).

In Dubai, the architectural design is exactly the same, just bigger: a tower, a mall, a water feature. Such are the common-places of these urban utopias, the basics of every mixed-use commercial real estate project.

BANGKOK

TO TRAVEL like 85 percent of tourists. Switch on a computer or
a tablet. Spend an hour or an hour and a half on the website of
some travel agency going through slide shows: hotel rooms (dominant colour, white or beige), gorgeous landscapes (dominant colours,
blue, sand), spas (zoom in on the soft contours of a woman's moist
back, hot stone massage, candles, bathtub full of rose petals).
Hesitate. Purchase a 2,500-euro package, per person, half-board.

Spend a few lunch hours in a fast-fashion place not far from
where you work, selecting a bathing suit or maybe several, some
good sandals, a nice pair of shorts, a couple of flowy linen vacation outfits. Spend six weeks on a diet or in a gym, doing group
Pilates focused on the lower body. Smear thighs and buttocks
with anti-cellulite cream every day. Resort to magazines to learn
five novel ways to tie on your beach wrap. Travel, consume.

Pack your new clothes in a large suitcase, bought especially for
the occasion, and launch yourself into a climate, into a luminous
space, into an Instagram pose that says, "On the beach I am superb."
À propos of Instagram, take a photo of the open suitcase, run it
through a vintage filter, and post it on social media, #travelling.

The sound of a suitcase towed over the fake marble floor of
the airport. A selfie in front of the departures screen, as a couple
or in a group of friends. Check in, a selfie, security check for carry-on,

a selfie, wander through duty-free. Result: three idiotic magazines, a long-lasting moisturizing cream, sun-protection hairspray, a fruity perfume, flowery, something light for the vacation. Boarding, please turn off your electronics, taking off, floating, inflight entertainment, floating, inflight shopping, floating, landing. Bringing your cellphone back to life, and then...the 3G network doesn't have the same name or the same cost. This is where elsewhere starts.

Selfie, #passportcontrol, selfie, #baggagehall, selfie, #taxi. Happy there will be Wi-Fi in the hotel. Sort the photos you've already taken this trip, notice a palm tree, catch it on the fly through the window, road-trip effect. Play around with some filters, think about the best hashtags, arriving. Check in, smiles, Wi-Fi connection, the sound of the suitcase rolling along, softened by the carpet, smiles, silence. The room looks a little like the photographs. The bathroom is a surprise. Upload a couple of photos on Facebook, wash up after the trip, count the *likes* after you come out of the shower and are resting on the king-size bed in your dressing gown. Travel, be a cliché.

◌ Suvarnabhumi, the international airport of Bangkok, an ambience of middle-class holidays coming to an end. The tourists here all have the same skin (SPF 30), the same batik accessories, the same souvenirs that look just like what was in the slide shows of the travel agencies. Images create the images, which create conformism, which creates the images.

In 2012, 53 million passengers came through this airport, the sixth largest in Asia, sixteenth in the world, a hub that all day every day distributes ordinary people from everywhere to the most beautiful beaches on the Andaman Sea and the Gulf of Thailand. In that year, Suvarnabhumi was deemed the most Instagram geotagged place on earth, coming in just ahead of the Siam Paragon shopping centre in Bangkok and Disneyland in California.

This strange record, only ever set in that one year, was never questioned, and you can speculate whether it was because tourists like showing they're in Thailand because Thailand is a "dream" destination, or because some Thai communications system operator set up a contest that allowed people to win nice little prizes, like a convertible, for posting a selfie geotagged in the Bangkok airport. It will forever remain one of the dense though derisory mysteries of the history of the internet.

☼ At this point in my travels, my hypothalamus has given up. Circadian rhythm, hunger, sleep, emotions…I no longer have an internal compass, my blood pressure is low, I feel cold. There's a dull, diffuse aching feeling, a wish to curl up in a hole in the ground or, in the absence of such a place, to break something, smash someone's face, a tourist's, for instance.

I spend seven hours in this sort-of shopping centre from which airplanes also take off, telling myself that if there were a category of airports most suited to long-term stays (useful for people like Edward Snowden and Mehran Nasseri), then Bangkok would defi-nitely not be on that list.

The departure terminal looks like a giant greenhouse, recti-linear and criss-crossed by moving sidewalks, where shopping areas are lined up in thematic order. The presence or absence of moving walkways has been determined in such a manner that travellers are forced to make their way through certain sectors on foot, notably those selling European luxury goods and duty-free stuff. I walk fifteen minutes in one direction, then ten minutes in another direction, then another fifteen minutes in yet another direction, before I finally find a place to buy a plain bottle of water.

As airport fashion requires these days, everyone moves around with a little pushcart. Huge advertising screens predominate, peddling perfume, regenerative serum with hyaluronic acid additives, and Kinder chocolate eggs. At certain points in the big corridor, gilded pagodas have been set up that sell Thai handicrafts made specifically for the captive clientele: expensive, serialized productions.

In the centre of the structure, a large, long, gold-coloured sculpture portrays a scene from Hindu cosmology: the churning of the ocean of milk. On one side is the team of gods, on the other the team of devils, each one tugging on a snake as though it were a rope and trying to overturn part of a mountain resting on the back of a turtle. Overlooking the scene from on high is a purple Vishnu with four arms. After a thousand years of effort, it says on a little plaque that summarizes the myth and that nobody reads, the ocean of milk ends up giving birth to a whole bunch of things, among them the nectar of immortality for which the gods and the demons have been battling (final winner, the gods).

Before this imposing sculpture, in which each of the twenty protagonists made of fake gold and wearing a pointy hat has more-or-less human dimensions, a crowd of tourists in shorts is taking selfies. Some are using their cellphones, others their tablets, which is even more ridiculous. They all try to frame their image in such a way that they appear alone in front of the installation. In the background, depending on the angle they find, will be either a Gucci or a Dior logo.

◌ I sleep for an hour in a shabby little lounge area, on a bench covered in vinyl with torn corners, my backpack as a pillow and my jacket pulled over my head as though over a birdcage to impose silence. I am shivering in this spot next to a vent that is churning out conditioned air. Instead of sinking into sleep, I am engulfed in a gummy sadness, the exhaustion of being homeless for the last two weeks merging with my current substantial disgust at the civilized world in general. I am beginning to develop a kind of anxious hatred of fake marble floors and glass ceilings. At this particularly wretched stopover, I have reached the physical and psychological limits of my capacity to resist the absurd. This gloom will stay with me.

After covering my legs and feet with the wrinkled and rather smelly stole that was once my scarf, I end up falling asleep. If

I could also cover up with large sheets of cardboard, it would demonstrate to what extent I have become a shopping centre tramp, an almost dissident condition that has something noble about it.

I surface later, with one cheek marked by the seams in my backpack, and it takes me a good minute to realize where I am. Around me, anyone who isn't pushing one of those little carts has their face stuck to a screen. Across from me, a couple of American college students, tanned and wearing denim mini-shorts and flimsy tops with flowy patterns, haven't bothered to take off their sunglasses.

I no longer feel like talking. Just the thought of addressing someone makes me feel sick, saying that I'm a journalist, that I'm interested in them and I'm wondering what brought them here, because none of that is true anymore. I no longer like people. I find them passive. Why don't they just refuse those pushcarts? Why don't they just switch off their screens for a while? Why don't they look around, just to see that what they're being offered in life is not acceptable?

In the 1960s there were already serious concerns about the future of this humanity that is so stupidly consumerist; there were questions about how meaningful a materialist life can be, and about the salaries that chain people to their role as shoppers, mere targets for the producers of manufactured goods.

Nowadays, the world over, those who have finally been granted access to leisure activities, vacations, cellphones, and luxury handbags through economic growth can feel happy in the midst of the domineering mindlessness of the image, in the completely hackneyed life purveyed by magazines and advertising leaflets (which have in fact merged, but that's another issue). The consumption of those publications feeds the growth, which feeds the possibility of even more consumption.

I look around me, and I see nothing more to criticize. People already said it all half a century ago. I am obsolete in my anger,

minuscule in my disgust, powerless on the shoulder of a global
highway where the pushcarts keep rolling by.

DUBAI

THE PERSIAN GULF, indigo blue, oil blue. Below the sea of oil
are the hydrocarbons. In the sky that extends the gulf, light rays
pick out tiny cross-shaped silhouettes zipping along, leaving a
vapour trail, blinking fuselages heading for Dubai International
Airport. In 2014, more than 70 million people transited here,
coming from and heading to the 260 cities of the world.

My mauve-tailed A330 sets its passengers free via one of the
glass appurtenances in Terminal 1. A ballet of orange flashing
lights dances across the tarmac in the mist. About two dozen
women, who I at first take to be a group of cousins, arrive with
me on flight TG517; in reality, this is a load of unskilled labourers
from a specialized employment agency in the Philippines. The
women are between twenty and thirty years old, with coppery,
thick-lipped faces, in simple clothes, their black hair pulled back
in ponytails. In Dubai they will do housework as cleaners and
nannies, or work as supermarket cashiers, waitresses, or cleaning
personnel.

The one I talk to as we wait to go through passport control
calls me "Ma'am," punctuating each of her short utterances with
this carefully learned, deferential appellation that embarrasses
me terribly. How can you have a normal conversation, ask simple
questions with no strings attached, make a joke, or just empathize

with someone who ends every reply with "Ma'am"? It is really quite impossible. And this impossibility signals the perverse nature of the system that employs and underpays these women. Imported to the Emirates as a domestic worker, the woman I speak with seems to have assumed the sub-proletarian identity assigned to her in the underbelly of globalization, to such an extent that she unwittingly prohibits herself from talking to anyone who doesn't share her fate as an equal.

This "discomfort of civility" haunts me every day I spend in Dubai, where the tourists, of which I am one, are called "Ma'am" or "Sir," as though the hard currency they have, which makes the bloated system of hotels, restaurants, and businesses go round, provided them with the same superior status that the members of the tribes living off the oil have laid claim to, those men dressed in white and gold, those women with their kohl-rimmed eyes, entirely veiled in black.

The particular form that tourism takes in Dubai mixes luxury and social domination, and harks back to a feudal hierarchy where pleasure is only taken in the servility of the other.

☼ I wake up after a short sleep on the fifty-fifth floor of Rose Rayhaan, a four-star establishment that a few years ago could claim the title of tallest hotel in the city, at least for several months. The bay window across from my bed opens up onto a science-fiction dawn, with skyscrapers emerging one by one from the bluish-pink pallor of the desert. A canopy of concrete and glass. To my right, less than two kilometres away, is Burj Khalifa with its 828 metres of verticality, architectural elegance, and functional aberration, blinking away in limbo so that airplanes can take note. Where the day is starting, the Persian Gulf, far away, is little more than a cloud.

An hour goes by in the warm, deluxe comfort of my bed. Motionless, I watch the spectacle of shadows hardening and forms taking shape, the sun extracting itself from the mists and dissolving them. Suddenly the horizon is filled with houses as far as the eye can see. Small cranes loom in the distance, right out into the gulf.

Closer by, on the other side of the highway, attached to a tower diagonally across from the one I'm in, is a billboard advertising Breitling, a watch brand founded in 1884 in the Swiss Jura Mountains; it covers four floors of windows and the entire breadth of the façade.

○ "Build it big and they will come" is what Sheikh Mohammed bin Rashid Al Maktoum, the Emir of Dubai, said when he had the biggest shopping centre in the world constructed at the foot of the highest tower in the world.

I am planning to spend four whole days in Dubai Mall.

The building is two metro stops away from my hotel, at the foot of Burj Khalifa, which shall be my beacon. The morning is fresh; I decide to walk.

There I am, on the road, which is actually a street, but so wide that two forty-ton trucks can easily pass each other. The ground is of no value. Huge interstitial spaces separate the towers, flat, useless, and neglected, that no pedestrian ever sets foot on and no architect has ever bothered to think about.

With the exception of the skyscrapers that have emerged in disorder, all structures are yellow. Yellow, the colour of the desert, somewhere between beige and mustard. Compact sand become commercial real estate. Twenty years ago there were only sand dunes. Now there is the Sheikh Zayed Road, an eight-lane highway, a river of asphalt irrigating the desert, along which roll German sedans and Italian sports cars, and on whose banks sprout these yellow buildings whose architecture inexorably expresses some aspect of the void.

This particular yellow is reminiscent of other deserts, aesthetic and urban deserts, deserts of inspiration, deserts in the middle of the desert.

Since nobody walks in the open air here, the sidewalk suddenly ends, continuing as a sandy path hardly wider than a human body, that leads between an empty lot and the highway for about 200 metres and brings me to another enormous empty parking lot on the edge of an office zone. From there, still minus a sidewalk, I walk along the decorative strip of grass that separates the two parts of the highway. Risking my life, I cross over to follow a hedge on the other side.

In the perfect world that Dubai claims to be, the highways are lined with trees and green spaces. Irrigated with drinking water made with fossil fuels, these decorative patches of green are a nonsense that nobody notices. Who in this era of touchscreen pleasures will look out the tinted windows at the landscape flowing by while ensconced in the back of a chauffeur-driven car?

One day, from the window of a taxi, I see an Indian labourer asleep on this highway lawn, using his hardhat as a pillow, and three Filipino women having a picnic there.

◌ The January sun, close to its zenith, is merciless on the eyes, radiating razor blades of light. Putting out only the effort I need to walk calmly through a cloud of exhaust fumes and an area built to the scale of cars, I arrive at the edge of Dubai Mall soaked in sweat.

To my right, Emaar, the government real estate company, is in the process of constructing a new ultra-deluxe hotel whose skeleton of steel and concrete slabs is already twenty storeys high, rising behind large palisades covered with advertising for French luxury goods. The sidewalk around the building site is already in place, its paving stones of green and ochre granite an exact imitation of shopping centre floors. No one will ever set foot on this non-air-conditioned outdoor space, since a carpeted glass tube will provide a comfortable connection from the hotel to the mall. From the height of this walkway, the view will be impeccable and the sidewalks will look sumptuous, for as Sheikh Mohammed bin Rashid Al Maktoum also said, "Everything here must be world class."

Proof, if it were necessary, that this sidewalk is not expecting a single person to walk on it is that it does not even lead to an entrance at Dubai Mall. I cross the road and enter an underground parking lot, where I keep moving straight ahead, since there is no sign indicating where to go. Finally I see a glass cage, shining in the half-light, from where two elevators and an escalator depart.

One floor up, I start down an nondescript corridor, a sort of service entrance for chauffeurs and servants, which takes me to a wide, luminous main artery, full of life and lined with boutiques and high-end shops. I have arrived. Small wonder that to my right I see Tommy Hilfiger; straight ahead, Zara Home, Liu Jo, Adolfo Dominguez, and Victoria's Secret.

To my left, a Costa Coffee (the other Starbucks). I decide to have a belated breakfast here and take one of the armchairs on the black wood "terrace" that overlooks the "street." I order a pastry whose pseudo-French name I have already forgotten (a puff pastry turnover full of chocolate chips) and a very foamy and caramel-sweetened café au lait, an American concoction whose name suggests some Italian origin.

How can I tell that I am no longer in Kuala Lumpur, and not on some exoplanet colonized by a nouveau-riche demiurge? A scent of rose is in the air. The spaces, atriums, and corridors are much bigger than anywhere else I know. A feeling of sustained luxury emanates from this voluminous palace because of the richness of the materials used in the construction and the intelligence—yes, intelligence—of the layout.

After a few days of wandering around Dubai Mall, I have to admit that, objectively, it is a very successful, if not exemplary, building of this genre and makes a positive impression. At the heart of its hugeness, everything is shiny and nothing is tacky. The walls, the floors, the ceilings, everything is very expensive, and this is obvious without being showy. And then there is the absolute cleanliness of each square centimetre of this colossal structure, ensured by an army of cleaning women imported from the Philippines.

Basically, you just have to love shopping to come here and feel good.

○ There is only one proper way to arrive at Dubai Mall, and that is in a chauffeur-driven car. You get out of the vehicle on Grand Drive, the warehouse zone that runs along the northeastern façade, parallel to Financial Centre Road. That is where four monumental doorways, about fifteen metres high, are lined up in all their extravagance, providing access to Galeries Lafayette to the east and Bloomingdale's to the north. Between these two points, a spectacular rotunda leads into the Grand Atrium, where events, exhibitions, and prestigious shows take place. Off to one side, a gigantic luminous parallelepiped in the style of an Arab fortress, with arched doorways on all four sides, takes you into the Souk, a sanitized version of the traditional Middle Eastern market.

Never having arrived in either a taxi or a limousine, I have not yet entered via one of these four huge doors. But I have several times taken the interminable 820-metre-long glass footbridge that links the metro station to the second floor of the shopping centre—an access point that is not without meaning, given the social hierarchy and the economic logic that rule Dubai Mall.

This floor was, in fact, conceived for middle-class families. Here you find multiplex cinemas, electronic game stations, amusement parks, access to the aquarium, fast-food restaurants, as well as small shops selling sweets or cellphones, stores for home appliances/CDs/DVDs/books, children's clothing, drugstores, low-cost perfumeries, and even walk-in medical clinics. The second floor is definitely the less noble one: it is meant for those who travel by metro. But it is no less lucrative. Spending considerable amounts of money on junk food and entertainment, families are the cash cows of shopping centres.

It is wise to remember that crowds, much like water, tend to flow downward, as A. Alfred Taubman, one of the fathers of the American shopping mall, said. Architects who know the classics thus tend to have the parking lots and metro access points come out on the second floor, from where the consumers can spread like magma into the lower floors.

○ In the window of a cellphone store I spot an iPhone case with a portrait of Sheikh Mohammed bin Rashid Al Maktoum made of a mosaic of diamonds. The price is not marked, but when I ask a salesperson I discover it costs 1,300 dollars.

Even before he became ruler of Dubai in 2006, "Sheikh Mo" was one of the most powerful men in the Middle East. His ambitions and his megalomania have provided his city with the look of today, both admirable and detestable, central and domineering.

This heir of the Al Maktoum clan has turned his emirate into one of the world's most important air travel hubs, a world trading port, a first-class tourist destination, and a fiscal paradise for the Arab-Muslim world. His "strategic visions" for Dubai and the United Arab Emirates resemble five-year plans infused with ultra-liberal voluntarism. Everything undertaken under his aegis is gigantic, luxurious, and runs counter to nature.

Sheikh Mo can be located somewhere between a benevolent dictator in power by divine right and a CEO-guru who, however, continues to be the father of a tribe of postcard Bedouin, a collector of women and racehorses, a falconer, and an occasional poet-philosopher, all at a scale compounded by cash.

○ Back in the fifty-fifth storey of the Rose Rayhaan hotel. A night view of the lights of a phantasmatic city. I could be the heroine of a wonderful movie; all I would need to do is get drunk in the hotel bar and meet Bill Murray.

Far below, Sheikh Zayed Road is an orange ribbon with red streaks that grow faint with speed. All around me, skyscrapers like dominoes twinkle from their windows.

A panorama of supernatural beauty. It makes me think of *Blade Runner*, *Metropolis*. It makes me think that nothing beautiful can ever happen to me again that has not already been caught on a lens. In films, catalogues, magazines, in a flow of shared images, with the eye of Google. There is no image that is virgin before Dubai at night. I walk in the footsteps of millions of tourists who have all been amazed by the same scene, have all taken the same photo, have all posted on the same social media. It's all a déjà vu, life lived vicariously.

It's 10:30. I'm hungry. The club sandwich on the room service menu strikes me as disgustingly conformist. I head out. I walk, my heart pumping, my nerves in search of resistance, like a predator in the fleeting glow of headlights. I am looking for the underbelly, danger, the usual grubbiness of a city at night, the pedestrian streets, the arches of bridges, the drunks and druggies, the tramps, the beggars. But there is no underbelly in Dubai. Under the sand, there is only oil money.

◌ I step into a Lebanese restaurant that looks like a Swedish sushi bar. On the ground floor, high tables and chairs in a fake light wood patina purvey a pseudo-artisan quality. On the shelves, various decorative objects in acid-bright colours supply the finishing touches for a contemporary look. One floor up there is a change of scene, an Oriental look. Wide benches line the walls, upholstered with cushions. A touch of modernity, as in *Elle Déco*, is provided by low metal tables in the style of recycled industrial waste. As though the ambitious Palestinian owner of this franchise (because it is one) had gone in search of old train cars in some abandoned northern European train station to fashion these low, characterful tables. There is no sense of form or materials here.

This late in the evening the restaurant is still busy. Beside me is a young Saudi family: seven entirely veiled women and a young man in blue jeans with sunglasses perched on his head. In a stroller between their table and mine a little girl, who must be the same age as my son, is asleep. Like him, she has long black eyelashes and cheeks like peaches. I can't take my eyes off her, unaware of how this might disturb her mother. I would love to take this little one in my arms, just for a moment feel the dense heat this little body of thirteen or fourteen kilograms gives off, asleep and feeling completely safe.

Not long ago I could look at children with perfect indifference. But the moment I had one of my own, fed him every day and saw him develop, the simple feeling of giving love in mutual dependence became a vital part of myself, a tremor that can be transferred to anything with a similar form when the object of my love is absent. I am a mother without her child: a heart overflowing with milk.

○ The Persian Gulf, royal blue in the vertical sunlight. The sun illuminates a flotilla of graceful triangles with finely edged tips, bending to their great lengths. White sails on dhows out in the open to make their fortune. They are pearl fishers.

The photograph, coloured by my imagination, dates from before the 1930s. Boats and divers were numerous though tiny in the immensity of this corner of the Indian Ocean, begging the sea to provide a living, pay the debts, feed a family for one more season. In Dubai as in many other parts of this hostile coast, where the sun makes the sea evaporate and dries the salt, the population for a long time sought their subsistence in the capricious innards of benthic bivalves.

Carried by the economic development of British India, certain clans of the Bani Yas tribe took up the pearl trade as a viable alternative to the cultivation of date palms. In the eighteenth and nineteenth centuries, nomadic people settled along the coast or established themselves there from May to September, the pearl season, before returning to their travels with tents and camels in the mountainous regions of the Arabian desert.

Is the pearl fisher a romantic figure? The image: with muscles tensed under skin that has been burnt by the sea, this is someone who is getting ready to drop down twenty-five metres, a nose clamp in place and a rock attached to his ankle as a weight. He will spend a minute to a minute and a half in the dense, saline darkness, holding his breath, harvesting oysters from the reef with his fingers in leather gloves so he can break the cement that holds them in place. What he harvests will be deposited in the boat. Others will open up the molluscs. They say you have to open up a thousand kilos of oysters in order to find three or four of the little mother-of-pearl pods. The ton of dead oysters is dumped back into the sea, and the income from the pearls is distributed to the entire team, pro-rated according to their merit and the social hierarchy.

The diver dives up to thirty times in a day. Sometimes when he comes back up he loses consciousness, he suffers lesions on his eyes from the pressure, and sometimes he does not return at all, drowning because of some technical problem. Often, for the four-month pearl-fishing season, he will have left wives, children, and aged parents behind in the desert. The family's subsistence is guaranteed by a loan from the operator. If the harvest is poor, the diver who has survived is in debt until the next season.

The trade in pearls created a position for Dubai in the global economy. It did not provide a fortune. Set up as a free port in the early twentieth century, the fishing village of the Al Maktoum clan, located at a crossroads for the trade in goods between Orient and Occident, saw its population grow thanks to the prospect of tax-free profits. A new class of business people, who were often more educated than those from the desert, established themselves and prospered, people from Iran, Iraq, Lebanon, Palestine, from the entire territory around the gulf, as far away as Balochistan.

As a central point in East–West trade, Dubai also suffered setbacks because of this international exposure, and in the 1930s was caught between two fires. Blowing in from Wall Street, the wind of the financial crisis tarnished fortunes and sources of credit, while in Japan, an industrial-biological miracle was taking place that made the price of pearls drop dramatically and definitively. Somewhere between Tokyo and Osaka, on an island in the warm waters of Ise Bay, the son of a noodle vendor, who dreamed of attaching strings of pearls to the necks of all the women of the world, invented oyster farming, signalling bankruptcies for the businessmen of Dubai.

Ever since the Al Maktoum clan arrived in Dubai, it has relied on the liberalism of regulatory and tax regimes for its growth strategies, all the while bringing in clever merchants and cheap labour. This was its saving grace in the crisis of the 1930s and is what has made its fortune right to the present day. In my eyes, Dubai in 2014 is nothing but the bloated version of an economic, social, and political construct, grown obese from its oil income, that hasn't evolved in over a century, though these facts are concealed behind a façade of modernity in erection.

⟲ At the heart of the Dubai Mall, 300 sharks and rays turn round and round in an aquarium that is fifty metres long and twenty metres wide. They move in the company of 32,700 other marine creatures, whose identity is of no interest to the communications people of the shopping mall. Strangely, the aquarium of Dubai Mall is not the biggest in the world. However, it does contain the greatest collection of tiger sharks.

The mere presence of these big predators means that those visitors who feel the plexiglass tunnel through the aquarium is not exciting enough can buy tickets to swim with the sharks, behind glass. Various options are on offer: you can go snorkelling in a cage, use a submarine scooter (with one or two seats), do a free dive with an oxygen tank, or do a cage dive with a tank, all with or without a guarantee that you will come close to a shark (the option with a guarantee requires the aquarium personnel to drive the sharks toward the tourists using bait, an operation that is, of course, more costly). Some of these offers do not require the tourist to know how to swim or even get their hair wet, and it is always possible to rent a GoPro camera in order to create an unforgettable souvenir of this moment of osmosis with nature.

☼ We are sharing a corner of a lounge in the ground-floor jewellery section that is inundated with waves of Wi-Fi. Four potted boxwoods mark the corners of a sand-coloured rug. Our square black leather armchairs are separated by a small white table. She has a laptop balanced on her crossed thighs. Her long brown curls have been rolled into a shiny chignon; she is wearing "nude" lipstick and a fashionable perfume, maybe Cinema by Yves Saint Laurent. She is completely engrossed by the Facebook interface that spreads across her fifteen-inch screen. I look at her, her twenty-year-old body, straight back, and perfect proportions sheathed in modern clothing, a turtleneck top, slim-legged pants, narrow waist, deploying all the means of seduction. But behind her glasses, her eyes, lost on the trail of her trackpad, can't open up to the opportunity for a conversation.

When I interrupt her, K. is very pleased to meet me. We speak French; she is Moroccan. She takes off her glasses, as though they were a barrier, as though they prevented me from seeing her bat her eyelashes. My work as a journalist makes her think for a moment that she might become a celebrity.

Three years ago, K. was recruited to work as a flight attendant for a company running private jets out of Dubai. It was operated by an Egyptian who subsequently went bankrupt. Unwilling to return to Morocco, she has been taking on various temporary jobs as a hostess in order to extend her residence permit.

K. likes spending her free time at Dubai Mall rather than in the small apartment she shares with another young woman her age. At the mall, she feels she is living in an important place, a central, multicultural environment where anything might happen, especially love and the fortune she thinks it will bring. She is twenty-four years old, not twenty, and is afraid she is no longer nubile, past her best-before date, and she would love to have children.

We have stayed in touch on Facebook. And I have been observing her from a distance as she hides her loneliness in group photos, surrounded by occasional colleagues or quickly forgotten girlfriends, striking a victory pose in front of a stand promoting real estate, or a Christmas tree, or a limousine.

○ Fine sand is stuck in between the soles of my feet and my sandals. Try as it might, Dubai cannot escape the desert. The rock dust transported by the wind powders the shoulders of the roads, lies in small heaps between the slabs of marble or in a fine grit on the sidewalks.

I am a European tourist. I come from the continent that invented tourism. I think that the tourism I practise—on foot, cultural, eco-aware—is the only worthwhile kind. I think my way of life—urban, with access to bicycle paths and green areas—is the only worthwhile kind.

I scrape up as much understanding and empathy as I can for the locals here, who for a long time experienced little else but thirst, and who today, quite naturally we are told, aspire to luxury in its most stereotypical form. But I don't really succeed. I can't adapt. I persist in behaving as though I were privy to the only true way of being in the world. I walk, risking my life. I cross highways on foot. Especially in the evenings, when I'm tired, I curse this town, this dream of a nouveau-riche camel driver, this development model that is the exact opposite of good sense.

○ It is an understatement to say that Dubai has a strange relationship with fresh air. While none of the sidewalks are meant to be walked on, the most popular restaurants in Dubai Mall are those with an outside terrace overlooking the famous dancing fountain. In this spot, which is reputed to be one of the hottest places on the planet, with temperatures of 40 degrees Celsius most of the year, the romantic practice of terrace-dining is called "dinner al fresco." A label that is not as much of a spoof as it sounds, since the exterior spaces are air-conditioned.

From the lower ground level, you reach the always crowded terraces through revolving doors whose function is to limit the exchange of conditioned air from inside and conditioned air from outside. But these doors present a problem; they often get blocked, especially when the place is busy.

In the enclosed space of one such revolving door, I get stuck for a few minutes because of a fat American wearing a trucker hat who had to force his way in. A very red-faced gentleman and his wife are seriously worried that we might run out of oxygen. They're probably in their sixties, and like 99 percent of the French tourists I have observed abroad, they talk too loudly and say stupid things (at least I consider them stupid). They are with a younger though much balder man, whose Ralph Lauren polo shirt and Rolex watch are signs of a life that is superior to theirs. This person uses English to make mocking remarks to me about the woman who, I later learn, is his mother-in-law.

The fact that, against my better judgment, I respond to them in French triggers a clingy sort of friendliness. When we finally get out of the revolving door trap, we sit down for a milkshake on the air-conditioned terrace.

R., the man with the Rolex, controls the conversation and uses this modest little occasion to demonstrate the natural interpersonal skills that, in the past, have been the basis of his "business" fortune. At Dubai Mall, he is playing the role of tour guide for his in-laws from France, who have come to see their grandchildren. Monsieur and Madame C. find the mall "very nice" and "really big." As a local by adoption, R. knows the place by heart from coming here so often with his wife and children. "There's not much else to do in Dubai."

R.'s wife is a wealth manager at BNP Paribas. Less than a year ago, when they were living near Geneva, the bank offered her a promotion, along with a lavish "expat package," to pursue her work in creative tax environments in Dubai. At the time, R. was directing a company dealing in gypsum and high-end plasterboard (mouldings, false ceilings, and sound insulation) that serviced clients in the luxury hotel business and the watchmaking industry. Since their arrival in Dubai, R. has no longer been working. He doesn't look after the children or the household either; the labour of several Filipino employees was part of the BNP Paribas deal. What does he do all day? Sometimes he takes his vintage car and roars up to Abu Dhabi at 160 kilometres an hour for a change in conditioned air. The rest of the time he kills time on the web.

A few weeks after our meeting, R. sends me a photo of his in-laws in an email attachment. They are not smiling as they pose in front of a Dubai Mall stand promoting Nikon cameras. The image, which has been run through a series of Japanese-made filters, is meant to be shared on social media, framed with a yellow border that says "I am at the heart of Dubai." Red-faced, double-chinned, and with blank stares, Monsieur and Madame C. are discovering a world where every human being can become a powerful marketing tool.

○ Walter Elias Disney was surely the most influential man of the twentieth century, and the first two decades of the twenty-first century have seen his aura mark the most diverse aspects of our existence. Well beyond the mouse called Mickey, this pioneer of American animation invented a form of storytelling that has been assimilated to the point of entering the subconscious of every specialist in political communication. He is also the father of the theme park, the immersive entertainment experience whose model has inspired the most prestigious museums of the world and numerous so-called classical cultural institutions. Within a span of fifty years, the "Disneyfication" of the world has reached proportions that exceed anything its admirers, as well as its detractors, could have imagined, showing up literally everywhere:

in a video clip advertising a tablet, at the annual general meeting of the investors of a large pharmaceutical company, in the speech of a candidate standing for election as president of a country, in an art exhibit dedicated to the grand masters of Impressionism, and so on.

Still, nowhere in the world is the spectre of Uncle Walt more present than in Dubai Mall. The dancing fountain, celebrated as the biggest in the world, owes much of its design and aesthetics to the movie *Fantasia* (1940), particularly the "Sorcerer's Apprentice" segment—at least that's what I think. At the beginning of the animated film, Mickey, the sorcerer's apprentice, falls asleep after ordering a broom to fetch water to fill a cauldron. In his dreams, the mouse is Moses on the mountain, and to the accompaniment of the symphonic poem by Paul Dukas, he lights up the stars and orders the waters to flow, just like Moses ordered them to part so his people could pass. Movies, and especially the films of Disney, are punctuated with these scenes where certain features that glorify the power of the heroine or the hero are emphasized by music. These images are imprinted on the collective imagination, especially that of the folks who design dancing fountains.

The one at Dubai was designed by Mark Fuller, an engineer who trained in the Disney theme park school in the 1970s, which makes him an "imagineer," a term coined by this school for someone who can recreate in real life a situation that was presented in a cartoon. His company, WET Design, has built more than 200 dancing fountains around the world, including one at Bellagio hotel and casino in Las Vegas (just across from the replica of the Eiffel Tower) and the one in the Morocco Mall in Casablanca. Shopping centres, hotels, and organizers of the Olympic Games are the main buyers of these spectacular objects.

At nightfall and right up to the closing of the shopping centre, the Dubai Fountain provides a five-minute show every half hour. A dense crowd collects at the edge of the small artificial lake and creates a cloud of blue screens reaching skyward. If you look for "Dubai Fountain" on YouTube, you can choose from among 300,000 different videos.

A few months after I returned home from Dubai, I watched *Frozen* (2013), Disney's version of Hans Christian Andersen's fairy tale "The Snow Queen," with a number of children. When Elsa decides to finally "let it go" in order to build an ice palace as she sings, it seemed to me that she was crystallizing the shape of an enormous dancing fountain. It made me think back briefly to Sheikh Mo, the man who also makes palaces emerge in the desert and water perform a dance in his glory.

○ *Come join the celebration in the skies of Dubai if you wish to*
     see people living in paradise.
Come render homage to Mohammed, the leader of Dubai,
     who knows that a branch can reach up to the sky
And hug the stars above. And if you're wondering how far his
     imagination can take us,
You can be sure that all this is insignificant compared to
     what he is planning and hasn't yet told us.
For Mohammed, Dubai is like a young girl he fell in love with,
     who through his mercy becomes the incarnation of pride.
He looks over Dubai like the sky itself in these sunny places
     and shaded spots, building for future generations who will
     carry our traditions.
He is a knight serving the "city of life." I pledge allegiance to
     him and promise him my sacrifice.

"Sama Dubai" is an ode to Sheikh Mo, sung by the Emirati singer Mehad Hamad. Every day at twilight the 200-million-dollar fountain dances to the syncopated rhythm of this hymn.

○ To travel, at least where I come from (post-1968 middle-class bohemia), is to encounter other ways of life, other tastes, other colours, and in the process experience the diversity and profundity of History. The sites one is absolutely meant to visit, and which tourist guidebooks extol, are often architectural remains of another era, another civilization, or they are places where you can participate in a form of social life that is typical for that region. Tourism of the sort I have practised according to what my parents taught me seeks to grasp something of both the past and the present in order to extract an alternative, other lifestyle, and can sometimes be called "exoticism."

Dubai completely evades this definition of tourism. The city offers nothing beyond the spectacle of its own present and the absolute comfort of universal conventions. Nothing the tourist has come to see in Dubai—notably the monumental architecture—is more than ten years old. That's excepting the sand, the sea, and the palm trees, which we mustn't forget were there well before they became mere signs of a successful seaside vacation.

In Dubai, a tourist will never have to adapt to a way of life that is different from their own, or to other leisure activities. Islamic practices and sharia law only really concern the locals of Dubai, while the law that applies to expat residents of Dubai or those passing through is the law of commerce, the universal religion of stereotypical luxury. At any moment of their stay, if they need food, tourists have a choice from among Lebanese, French, Italian, American, Chinese, Thai, Korean, Japanese, or Mexican restaurants. They cannot help but sleep in a king-size bed in a three-, four-, or five-star hotel that is part of some big international chain. Anything a tourist can buy here has been manufactured in China, Vietnam, or Bangladesh under a French, Swedish, or Spanish label.

Travelling as though you were channel-surfing. In this prefab framework, where nothing surprises or requires effort, at this crossroads of national stereotypes and theme parks, Dubai has invented tourism free of time and place, tourism like a bouquet of television channels. Everyone can find what they already know about the world confirmed in Dubai—no need to adapt, and no disappointment. Guaranteed return on the investment. In 2014, 11.6 million visitors departed Dubai with smiles on their faces.

◌ Before Dubai Mall came along to crush all the other shopping centres of the region with its superlatives, tourists in search of high-carbon-footprint sensations would go to the Mall of the Emirates. Ski Dubai, the famous indoor ski slope, is perched on stilts that are eighty-five metres high, constituting one of the most sinister theme parks I have ever had the pleasure to visit.

The total absence of natural light in this place increases the anxiety you feel at being in a post-apocalyptic capsule that is reconstituting what life on Earth was like before humanity was condemned to exile on Mars. This ambience of a space station in orbit is reinforced by the fact that nearly everyone is wearing the same clothes. The cost of admission lies somewhere between 50 and 130 euros and includes the price of a blue, red, and black ski suit, a pair of gloves, and a pair of boots.

Some clients, however, wear a different suit of clothes, usually more tight-fitting and more fashionable, and are a sort of aristocracy here. They are expats and hail from distant regions of the world that have mountains or a continental climate, where skiing is still a sport pursued in the open air (albeit with a carbon footprint that is not much lower, but that's another issue).

What mysterious reasons might there be for those who have experienced "real" winter sports to want to come and ski here? B., an IBM manager from Slovenia, who takes her two boys, aged seven and ten, skiing here once a week, explains, "In Slovenia, skiing is a tradition. I didn't want our expatriate life to prevent my children from making progress in this sport."

For a long time the geographical features of a region would shape the usages and cultures of the local population. By resorting to the magical power of fossil fuels to offset the sandy furnace that is Dubai, the city has set itself up as the universal aggregate of out-of-this-world experiences and practices. Today it is nothing more than a hollow place in the world where you are rich from giving up nothing.

I sometimes recall that, in the name of family entertainment, performing circus penguins who never see the light of day are raised in the basements of the Mall of the Emirates. For the equivalent of 340 euros, the park sells tourists the option to don a neoprene suit and spend ten minutes swimming with the penguins in their refrigerated aquarium. On days when I'm feeling sensitive, just thinking about this particular reality brings tears to my eyes.

◌ In the early twentieth century the Al Futtaim family grew rich in the pearl trade. After the financial crisis of the 1930s, the patriarch converted to importing Japanese cars. The clan, which is sometimes friendly and sometimes hostile to the Al Maktoum emirs, has always been one of the wealthiest in the region. Until he died in 2021, Majid Al Futtaim headed the third-largest fortune of the Emirates (the two larger ones being held by Khalifa bin Zayed Al Nahyan in Abu Dhabi and Mohammed bin Rashid Al Maktoum in Dubai).

Majid Al Futtaim was the man who brought snow and penguins to the desert. The conglomerate he directed specializes in real estate, shopping centres, family entertainment, and supermarkets. His activities were dispersed in the entire region that is under the influence of the Gulf states, from Egypt to Pakistan, which is where, among other things, he held the exclusive franchise for Carrefour supermarkets.

After the Arab Spring in Egypt, Majid Al Futtaim turned his promises to invest into a political weapon against the Muslim Brotherhood. His support for General Abdel Fattah el-Sisi was expressed via an array of shopping centres built between Alexandria and Cairo. In early 2017, Majid Al Futtaim inaugurated the Mall of Egypt, a high-end shopping centre fitted out with a ski hill just like the one in Dubai, in the new 6th of October City, on the outskirts of Cairo.

A joint venture uniting Majid Al Futtaim Group and the French company Veolia manages the energy required for the infrastructure of this leisure park—maintaining, for example, a constant temperature of minus 2 degrees Celsius in the 22,500-square-metre park and producing 25 tons of snow a day for 365 days of the year. Veolia, which trades on the stock market, has among its main shareholders Caisse des dépôts et consignations (French public funds), the industrial group Marcel Dassault, and an offshore Qatari government account based in Luxembourg.

◌ On the ground floor of the world's biggest mall is a Waitrose supermarket. In front of me at the checkout are three tall, blond, generously proportioned Russian women, two just past adolescence and their ageless-looking mother, all of them in full makeup and dressed in showy summer clothing—gold, coral pink, flowery patterns, their feet in French-label shoes. They are loud and they laugh as they unload a cart overflowing with food, including three cardboard trays, each holding thirty-six cans of Pepsi Light, onto the narrow checkout conveyor belt.

A petite Asian woman with coppery skin, maybe twenty years old, stands at the checkout to run the mountain of merchandise through a scanner, operating the moving belt with a foot pedal. The three Russian women don't even glance at her as she fills one sack after another, manoeuvring the trays of Pepsi with her short arms, stacking everything at her feet where a delivery service will collect it later. They chit-chat as they wait for a sum to show up on the digital screen and then extend a gilt credit card before they head off into the depths of Dubai Mall to end up, we can assume, at a table in a franchised coffee shop where they will use multicoloured straws to sip three caramel frappuccinos packed full of ice cubes and whipped cream.

The women cashiers at Waitrose work standing up, with one foot permanently poised on the pedal that activates the moving belt. They do not work in natural light. Their workday is ten hours with three short breaks. They are paid the equivalent of 350 euros a month.

On the surface, Waitrose is a high-end British supermarket chain, providing select groceries—fresh, organic, and fair-trade products. It is an official supplier to the royal family.

On the ground-floor level of Dubai Mall, the store bearing the Waitrose name is licensed to a Dubai company, Fine Fare Food Market, that is a front for Spinneys Dubai.

In every country of the Middle East and the Gulf region, the Spinneys supermarket chain belongs to the Abraaj Group, a stateless investment trust that is settled in one of the five free zones of Dubai and is under the direction of Arif Masood Naqvi, a Pakistani from Karachi who trained with Arthur Andersen in London. Only in the territory of Dubai does Spinneys—for some strange reason—belong to Ali Albwardy, a local polo player and retired owner of a vast and diversified conglomerate.

⟡ Before S. became a waitress in the restaurant where I order a tomato-mozzarella panini, she was a cashier for Waitrose. It is 3 p.m., I am her only customer, and she is cheerful, willing to talk. She tells me about her life.

Three years ago she left her village in the suburbs of Cebu in the Philippines to join the army of unskilled labourers who maintain the mirage of Dubai. She is absolutely enthusiastic about her job as a barmaid at Carluccio's (a shop that sports the slogan "Honestly Italian"). She is unbothered by the difficult schedule or the constant video surveillance. Her body, which is still young, does, however, remember the pain of the years at Waitrose. Her recent move up the social ladder has translated into two noteworthy material improvements: she's earning 50 euros more per month and she has a view of the dancing fountain from Carluccio's terrace.

At twenty-two years of age, S. is married and the mother of a three-year-old boy. Her husband, who is the same age, also works in Dubai, and she says they are lucky they can live together (albeit with four other people in a dormitory they rent from their employer, an hour by bus from Dubai). Their little boy has stayed in Cebu, in the care of the family, and is nothing but a smile on a cellphone, a memory inscribed in her body that occasionally lights up a Skype window.

The conditions of life that S. and her husband are experiencing place them in the upper segment of the unskilled workers imported to the Emirates; the Bangladeshi, Pakistani, or Nepalese construction workers win the prize for the worst conditions. Here, as in Aldous Huxley's *Brave New World*, the only developmental perspectives in regard to work, accommodation, or the possibility to be with your family are determined by the narrow constraints of the caste you come from: if you are deserving, you move up from cashier to barmaid. Bringing the family together is quite out of the question.

On Facebook, where she contacts me right after we meet, S. posts a lot of photos of what she eats—pistachio ice cream, fry-ups, and noodle soup; selfies with her husband; viral videos of "weird world happenings," usually of a sexual nature; and prayer texts such as "God, I would like to take a moment not to ask anything of you but to thank you for everything I have. (Please pass on the message if you believe.)"

Over the course of her posts, I also discover how much she truly likes Dubai. The day the city was named to host the 2020 World Expo, she took a selfie in front of the dancing fountain, ecstatic, as though, in some strange way, she were going to personally benefit from this international event in the place where she is exploited.

○ On the ground floor between New York and Paris (Bloomingdale's and Galeries Lafayette): a boulevard connects these two department stores, passing through two of the building's busiest atriums. In the game of Monopoly, this would be the most expensive street of the mall-city (with Fashion Avenue, the ultra-lucrative strip where the most prestigious fashion labels of the world would be concentrated). In Dubai Mall, the jewellers and watchmakers are located between New York and Paris. Herewith a small census of who is present.

On my left: Montblanc (the Swiss Richemont group), Baume & Mercier (Swiss Richemont group), the multi-label boutique Watch Gallery (Paris Gallery Group, owned by the Al Fahim family of Abu Dhabi), Richard Mille (Swiss watchmaker), the multi-label boutique Damas Les Exclusives (Damas group, of Syrian origin and based in Dubai). I note that the multi-label boutiques sell mainly Swiss watches.

On my right: A. Lange & Söhne (Swiss Richemont group), the multi-label boutique BinHendi Watches & Jewellery (BinHendi Enterprises, a Dubai group, owned by Mohi-Din BinHendi, the former director of airport customs in Dubai, then head of development of the civil aviation department, and chief administrator of development of the international airport and its duty-free shops), Pomellato (French Kering group, formerly PPR), Audemars Piguet (Swiss watchmaker), Glasshütte Original (Swiss Swatch group), Versace Jewellery (a franchise held by the Dubai group Samra), De Beers Diamond Jewellers (British joint venture with the Belgian holding company of French citizen Bernard Arnault and the Luxembourg conglomerate of South African De Beers mines, who bought out Bernard Arnault in early 2017 and currently owns 100 percent of the operation), Chaumet (Bernard Arnault's French LVMH group).

Around the main atrium, and occupying the spaces that are most visible from the main entrance: Tiffany & Co. (American jeweller), Graff (British jeweller), Breguet (Swiss Swatch group), Piaget (Swiss Richemont group), Rolex (Swiss watchmaker), Patek Philippe (Swiss watchmaker), Chopard (Swiss jeweller and watchmaker), Bulgari (French LVMH group), Cartier (Swiss Richemont group).

Continuing straight on, in the direction of "Paris," on my left: Pinctada (Dubai jeweller specializing in pearls), Van Cleef & Arpels (Swiss Richemont group), Korloff Paris (Morad Behbehani's Kuwaiti group), Al Fardan Jewels & Precious Stones (Qatari Al Fardan group). On my right: Levant Jewellery (property of Arif Ben Khadra, a Palestinian-Moroccan business agent acting on behalf of Israeli Lev Leviev), David Morris (British jeweller), the multi-label boutique Ahmed Seddiqi & Sons (owned by the Dubai Seddiqi family), Paspaley Pearls (Australian Paspaley group), Tabbah (Lebanese jeweller).

Around the circular atrium that opens onto the area labelled "Souk": Jaeger-LeCoultre (Swiss Richemont group), TAG Heuer (French LVMH group), Vertu (British manufacturer of luxury cell-phones assembled by hand by the Finnish group Nokia—declared bankruptcy in 2017), Longines (Swiss Swatch group), Zenith (French LVMH group), Omega (Swiss Swatch group), Mezgarzadeh (Iranian rug merchant).

I think this list requires no further commentary.

☼ In the part of the world I come from, mention of Dubai conjures up images of workers imported from the Indian subcontinent, deprived of their passports, and dying of loneliness on pharaonic building sites.

In the opinion of the citizens of Dubai and of a certain class of expatriates, a system that benefits everyone cannot be considered a scandal. "If the Sri Lankans, the Pakistanis, and the Filipinos didn't find what they were after, they wouldn't come to Dubai," says one such person, who works in the group that markets Dubai Mall. "They earn money here. At home, they wouldn't."

Spending a few days in Dubai means experiencing a world based on permanent inequality, where men and women, locals and foreigners—the foreigners from rich countries and those from poor countries—are not equal, not in their rights and not in the opportunities open to them. You may find that unpleasant, but it is the "Dubai system," to give a name to this openly iniquitous economic model, which is devoted to the profit of some via the voluntary submission of the others. It is, in fact, the system in which the vast majority of the world's population is immersed.

I am thinking of those who thrive and those who don't in the newly industrialized regions of the planet. Those who work mainly for extraterritorial powers, the offshore and tax-free multinationals. Those who do not live in our failing welfare states. In fact, about the whole planet.

So there is nothing exceptional about spending a few days in Dubai. It just means experiencing the world the way it is.

ISTANBUL

IN ATATÜRK AIRPORT in Istanbul, a gigantic Victoria's Secret shop is located right at the exit from security, one of the most visible commercial spaces in the international departures area. The boutique forms a half-circle next to the duty-free shop.

Besides lingerie, the store sells perfumes and cosmetics as well as a selection of items that are useful for travellers: toiletry kits, cellphone cases, wallets, and passport covers. This "sexiest brand in the world" has every reason to be located in an airport.

Everywhere on earth, Victoria's Secret uses the same colour scheme—black and pink—the same images, the same interiors. Lit-up advertising panels show extra close-up shots of young women's faces, always with long hair, their mischievous gaze firmly and confidently facing the camera. Giant screens run a constant parade of women in underwear and stiletto heels, a porn aesthetic of fast underwear fashion that has become the company's trademark.

Since the early 2000s, this manufacturer of lingerie, originally from California, has been aggressively pursuing a policy of international growth that has culminated in selling franchises to operators of duty-free shops in the most remote places. Along with Starbucks and McDonald's, it is one of the brands I have seen most often in the last month. Its success in Muslim countries nowadays, where I have observed numerous veiled women browsing its products, seems to indicate that the American version of woman-as-object is closer than one might think to the image disseminated by traditional Islam.

Atatürk Airport, the third-largest hub in Europe, offers one of the biggest duty-free spaces on the continent. The company managing these shops as well as Victoria's Secret is ATÜ. A joint venture, it brings together TAV, the operator of Turkish airports, and Unifree, a company specializing in managing duty-free stores that was founded with private Turkish capital but is controlled by the German group Gebr. Heinemann.

ATÜ not only runs the duty-free shops in all Turkish airports but also has the monopoly for duty-free in Tunisia, Georgia, Macedonia, and Kosovo. It is present in Oman, Saudi Arabia, Lithuania, and in Texas (at George Bush Intercontinental Airport, Houston). The feeling that all airports of the world look alike owes a lot to companies like ATÜ.

CASABLANCA

CASABLANCA, seen through the dirty window of winter; grey exhaust from the chimney pots has extinguished the city. By early morning, the wind from the Atlantic has dispersed the odours, punched holes in the sky, and dampened the dust. Along the coast-line, where the plastic garbage washes up, a paved boulevard offers an escape from the downtown traffic jams. To the left, fences around building sites indicate the imminent development of an amusement park here and luxury apartments with a view toward America there, anticipating by at least fifty years an economic growth, that, if it is shared equally, might allow an upper middle class to emerge. The road that leads to Morocco Mall is a herald of future promises.

○ It has something of a spaceship about it, a vessel that has run aground between two beaches. Seen from the sky, it resembles a giant suppository or a tampon, some pseudo-organic shape that reveals the builders' untalented and unintelligent intention to copy the supple and monumental architecture of Zaha Hadid.

When you approach from the northeast, the main entrance, at the foot of a glass portion of the façade, is hidden by a small windowless spheroid building that contains an IMAX 3-D theatre where you can see the latest American blockbusters for 70 dirhams a ticket. The side of the mall that stretches along the road is windowless, its rounded grey walls plastered with giant advertising. If the mosaic of LED screens that covers a big section of this wall worked and was lit up more often, it would give the whole thing a futuristic look.

A musical fountain runs along the west side of the building, with a very long stretch of stagnant water hiding the constellation of metallic points and underwater spotlights, currently under repair. A promenade leads past, and from here you can see the ocean, which on this particular day foams white over a soupy, jittery grey below a nervous sky. Plexiglass terraces punctuate the western façade of the mall along the entire length of the top floor.

Located within ten kilometres of each other on this same Atlantic coast, Morocco Mall and the Great Hassan II Mosque seem to have been designed to resonate with each other. Two temples, each of its own kind, claiming the same superlatives and justifying their dimensions by the influence they supposedly offer the economic capital of the country. "The biggest in Africa" apparently a much desired and much disputed label for both shopping centre and mosque.

Technically, Morocco Mall is a "destination" mall, the opposite of a community mall: it is not meant for the local population but counts on clients from farther away. A destination mall needs to offer young people, couples, or families who have undertaken the journey to get there at least a whole day of activity. Besides cinemas, such malls contain bowling alleys, aquariums, amusement parks, dancing fountains, skating rinks, wave pools, and ski hills (these last two items are not available at Morocco Mall, and the dancing fountain hardly ever works).

◌ At the end of a carpet that was once red, a row of glass doors opens onto a welcome counter with no welcome personnel. Palm trees grow out of the brown carpet. To the left is FNAC, across the way Brioche Dorée: we are in the zone of French influence, colonialism today. Beyond, two sinuous gut-like corridors lead away, bringing to mind the intestines of a whale lit up with neon tubes. Farther along is the central space with its ballet of escalators that lead to the open terraces and upper floors. In the middle is the gigantic aquarium. Behind that, Galeries Lafayette. That store occupies a building within a building, a rounded structure whose façades are covered with gold-and-silver-coloured metal plaques—an architectural move that won Morocco Mall a small citation in the *Guinness Book of World Records*, since this is the biggest store façade in the world that is located inside another store.

I go up for a coffee.

I encounter a man with a moustache, still wearing his hat, together with his wife, whose hair is also covered; they are in their inactive or post-active fifties, both seated at a table, his hand limply holding a cardboard cup from which dangles a Lipton's tea label. They are alone in this fast-food storey, listening to the silence that is interrupted here and there by distant echoes of voices rising from the first floor. They will not be buying anything. Nothing but the one cup of tea. "Everything is very expensive here," says the man. "We only came to look," says the woman.

Yes, but what is there to look at? On this second floor of the mall, the southwestern point where the restaurants are concentrated offers one of the most desolate aspects of globalization. Pizza Hut, Burger King, McDonald's, Domino's Pizza, KFC, brands that have become synonymous with cheap fast food, are selling their formulaic fare here for prices that transform it into exceptional moments for a majority of the Moroccan population. Has this couple of ordinary older Moroccans just come to view the spectacle of globalization rushing past?

○ I meet Madame M. in the first-floor washroom she is in the process of cleaning. We don't share a language, so the questions I ask her in French hang in the bleach-soaked air between two smiles. A little later I see her again at the edge of the parking lot. Encouraged by this second chance meeting, which she seems to think is lucky, she gestures for me to come along: not far, she knows someone who can act as interpreter.

We walk through a residential area that borders the mall. Single-family homes with swimming pools, laid out like in America, protected by high fences on one side and by a sleepy security guard in a kiosk on the street side.

Immediately adjoining, and backing right onto the pseudo-Californian villas, there is a slum, displaying its corrugated metal, its rags, and its parabolic antenna. Rivers of mud run in the ruts of the narrow streets. Children drop their ball games to swarm around us, and we make slow headway along the narrow, uneven paths.

Madame M. stops in front of the shanty of Madame H., who happily invites us into the six square metres of corridor she inhabits with her husband and three children. She speaks a hesitant school French. The little entrance slipway serves as both kitchen and bathroom and is separated from the living room by a curtain made of strips of plastic. She makes mint tea and brings out some semolina bread. Madame M. and her sister, whom she went to collect, are there too, and we take a seat on benches that are padded with cushions and blue-and-purple cloth. They line the walls of the corridor and also serve as the children's beds. In the middle is a long, narrow, low table where Madame H.'s oldest son, who is ten, is doing homework with a teenage cousin. We chat by the light of a bare bulb. The small motley interior space is intense, stark, and rigorously well-kept; every square centimetre counts and everything can be used for something else. The conversation is disjointed for lack of understanding.

Madame M. is employed on a weekly basis at Morocco Mall and cleans the toilets there for a handful of dirhams; she is the wealthiest of the three ladies. Her sister does some housework in the neighbourhood villas and so does Madame H., whose husband sells snails on the beach. Madame H. is not much more than thirty years old and is the only one who went to school for a few years, which is where she learned French and perhaps also acquired her belief in social mobility. Her children walk eight kilometres every day to go to the nearest school, and while others send their kids off to sell paper tissues on the side of the road, she is one of the rare mothers who has staked everything on education, bringing her niece in twice a week from a distant neighbourhood to do homework with her son, and speculating faithfully on hopes for a better future.

Like all the women I have seen in this neighbourhood, the three around me are wearing dressing gowns made of fluorescent polyester with Disney designs. Once again, globalization is present in this completely counterintuitive phenomenon that makes it cheaper for the poorest of the poor to wear clothes made in China rather than in their own environment. In China, where some employee of a textile factory made unauthorized copies of an image from *Frozen* or of Winnie-the-Pooh, ripping it off the internet and transferring it into a garish design reproduced on kilometres of fleece for mass export. At the other end of the container-ship line are these women, whose difficult lives don't prevent them from standing tall, yet whose dignity is betrayed by these absurd clothes imposed by the economic realities of free trade.

☉ I leave my hosts to return to the shopping centre, goodbyes without promises or a future. Behind the smiles lie torrents of expectations that were not expressed.

The muddy pathways widen into empty lots, and a little farther along the stench of public latrines floats in the air. One image dominates the horizon: a man with his right arm draped over the wide back of a low couch, encircling the shoulders of a woman with long blond hair. In front of them, amid pastel-coloured furniture, two children run by, whose love of life and energy are vividly portrayed by their blurred silhouettes. A boy and a girl, aged around six and eight. A bay window in the vast living room overlooks the ocean. In one corner, the outline of a big flat screen and a small stereo, a few magazines on a low square table and a Savoy-type vase. Beyond the children a big white rectangular table with six Eames-style chairs is lit up by two large globe lamp-shades. In the background there's an American kitchen.

The billboard image wasn't meant to be printed on such a large surface, so everything looks a little pixelated in this ad for a future housing complex, which is attached to the fence that hides a garbage dump on the edge of the slum. The ad serves as a net for the permanent soccer game the neighbourhood kids are engaged in.

In 2020, Casablanca will be a city without slums. The five-year development plan that was signed in 2014 announced that the remaining pockets of poverty, which often border the most high-end residential zones, would be removed. To this end, the authorities have to come to an agreement not only with the owners of the squatted territory but also with the slum-dwellers themselves. The owners figure that the removal, which is their responsibility, is too expensive and they refuse to pay. The slum-dwellers claim that the compensation they are offered is insufficient and that a relocation would penalize them because they earn their meagre income from activities they have developed in the neighbourhood (selling snails on the beach, doing housework for their rich neighbours, cleaning the shopping centre). Rumour is that these slums invariably grow on future construction sites, and that the squatters hope to extract money from the evictions they will suffer. Rumour is that the slums will not disappear from Casablanca any time soon.

○ In 2009, Davide Padoa won the International Property Awards prize for best architecture in the category "commercial property in the Arab region," honouring his work on Morocco Mall. In a photo taken in Dubai at the award presentation, he looks like an insurance salesman Tex Avery might have drawn. He is holding a framed certificate and has perfectly aligned teeth and curly hair, damp with emotion, stuck to his forehead. Behind him is the logo of the CNBC channel, which at the time was the main sponsor of the International Property Awards, one of some 200 such competitions in the world that honour real estate developers.

At his right, a very pretty young woman with carefully plucked eyebrows, her hair ironed straight, represents the Aksal group, which owns the mall. This is Miss L., head of communications, whom I meet in Casablanca. The photo doubtless shows her experiencing one of the high points of her career, since she has reframed it for use as her profile picture on a well-known professional social media platform.

Davide Padoa took courses in architecture in Italy and California and then became an expatriate in Indonesia. In Jakarta, where he spent the first years of his working life, he had ample time and opportunity to develop an aesthetic for the construction of oversized buildings in a tropical megalopolis. Jakarta is like Kuala Lumpur and Manila. When he established himself in London, he joined a company that specialized in the construction of shopping centres around the world. He signed off on the Odysseum in Montpellier, among other grandiose projects.

Like all developers of commercial property, Aksal paid to have Morocco Mall win the numerous prizes it flaunts today. An integral part of every marketing budget, the fees to participate in such competitions are high, but the categories for which one can apply are so numerous that each competitor can be sure to add a line or two to their Wikipedia page afterward.

The Aksal group is very pleased with Davide Padoa's work. They may hire him for the construction of another spectacular mall, this time in Rabat, one hour away by car in a country where 11 percent of the population lives on less than 20 dirhams (1.9 euros) a day. The presence of these two gigantic "destination" shopping centres targeting an upper middle class of shoppers speaks of economic planning that lies well beyond common sense.

○ In the last hours of winter, the lovely Ammelne Valley presents the most decorative, beautiful contrasts. Here and there grassy fields in brilliant emerald green extend, lighting up the pink ochre of the Lesser Atlas desert, with almond trees in white bloom waiting patiently in the fecund frost. The birdsong in these wondrous orchards is deafening.

With a little imagination, and simplifying a few things, you could toss some sepia images on the table and take the history of Morocco Mall back to Tafraout in the 1930s. There would be a young Amazigh boy in a white tunic, carrying a stick and leading a donkey. In the background, a group of women would be kneading the dough for semolina bread, their eyes hidden behind a fringe of silver medals.

Haj Ahmed Benlafkih could have been that boy, his donkey laden with the harvest of almonds he was taking to sell at the souk on instructions from his father, armed only with the knowledge a child acquires through mimicry and the basic math he needs for commerce.

As it so often is in the stories that begin like this, and that are getting just a little tiresome, little Benlafkih ended up making his fortune in business. Almonds, argan, dates, the fruits of the western Souss, sold in Casa; after that he diversified, import-export, hard-earned successes, catalyzed by ambition and good relationships. Finally, what really made Ahmed Benlafkih one of the great Moroccan capitalists was green tea imported from China, to which Moroccans add sprigs of mint and sugar. His wealth, accumulated during the reign of Hassan II, has benefited the third and now the fourth generation of his descendants. He is the grandfather of Salwa Idrissi Akhannouch, the owner of the Aksal group.

Salwa Akhannouch could have contented herself with being a rich heiress, marrying well, and producing three beautiful children, which she certainly did as the wife of Aziz Akhannouch, the extremely versatile minister close to Mohammed VI, and son of a capitalist

Berber like herself. But she chose to go into business with the aplomb and pride that we know are characteristic of the women of her region and her background, or that we ascribe to them.

I'd like to digress for a moment about Aziz Akhannouch, heir to a former Moroccan fuel distribution company, owner of the biggest network of gas stations in the country. Renamed Akwa, the family holding company worked throughout the 1980s to expand its interests in all directions, including telecommunications, media, property development, and hotels. In the early 2000s it was the main importer of hydrocarbons in Morocco, with 400 service stations, holding 24 percent of the gasoline and 34 percent of the natural gas markets. In 2004, Akwa joined with Mærsk (the biggest shipping company in the world) and obtained the rights to the first container terminal in the port of Tanger Med, a service station for freighters, located at the very entrance to the Mediterranean.

Now, what does Salwa Akhannouch do while her husband is pursuing a double career as government minister and billionaire? She takes an interest in ceramic tiles, floor coverings, and interior décor. Not as a private homeowner, but as a businesswoman, making the deals. This is the mid-1990s. In 2001 she buys her very first franchise and opens a La Senza lingerie boutique in Casa, then one in Tangier and a second one in Casa. In 2004 there is a real turn in her fortunes when she signs with Inditex, the giant Spanish textile business that includes Zara, a franchise that will make her (personal) fortune. The holding company she creates to manage her portfolio of brands is called Aksal.

She then begins collecting exclusive distribution deals in Morocco, first with Massimo Dutti, another Inditex brand, and then, aiming ever higher and pricier, with Dior and Fendi (LVMH group), then Gucci (PPR group). Boutiques open up everywhere, in Agadir, Marrakech, Tangier, and in the Mohammed V International Airport.

One day, probably around 2006 or 2007, she meets up with Faisal Al Jedaie, CEO of the eponymous Saudi group whose subsidiary company, Nesk, has recently specialized in the acquisition of fast-fashion franchises and is managing brands such as Mango, Promod, Call It Spring, Aldo, Stradivarius, Okaïdi, Parfois, Suite Blanco, Vincci, and Origem in Saudi Arabia, Jordan, Algeria, Egypt and Morocco. It is not hard to imagine that on that day Salwa Akhannouch and Faisal Al Jedaie had no problem at all finding a topic of conversation.

○ On December 1, 2011, the Aksal and Al Jedaie groups took great pleasure in inviting journalists and celebrities from around the world for the inauguration of "the biggest mall in Africa," or "the biggest mall in North Africa," depending on the mood and the nerve of the communications teams. Morocco Mall, the result of a joint investment of 2.7 billion dirhams (250 million euros), emerged after three years of construction. Under the usual glassed-in roof, without which a mall is apparently not worthy of the name, it consists of 250,000 square metres of white marble floors on three levels, and 350 stores, most of which are franchises held by the two collaborating groups.

Meanwhile, to realize her dream of building a mall in Casablanca "as beautiful as the one in Dubai," Salwa Akhannouch obtained concessions from Inditex for the rest of its brands, Bershka, Oysho, Uterqüe, Pull&Bear, and Zara Home, as well as other fast-fashion shops such as Banana Republic and Gap, luxury brands bearing the "polo" stamp such as Ralph Lauren and La Martina, M.A.C. cosmetics (Estée Lauder group), and above all the FNAC franchises (PPR group) and Galeries Lafayette.

FNAC and Galeries Lafayette are two of the mall's three anchor stores. The third one is the supermarket Marjane, which is 100 percent owned by Al Mada, formerly the Société nationale d'investissement, a trust that belongs to the royal family of Morocco.

Moroccan journalists were not allowed to attend the inauguration. On the day of the event they were blocked from getting on

the bus that was supposed to take them to the red-carpet celebration. A press attaché provided the surreal pretext that "the
international guests expressed the wish that they stay away."

⊙ Her Royal Highness Princess Lalla Meryem, the older sister
of King Mohammed VI, is wearing a red tartan suit Vivienne
Westwood may have designed. She cuts the green colour-of-Islam
ribbon at the entrance to Morocco Mall with a pair of scissors a
little girl wearing a tiara hands her. Behind her is a black marquee
studded with blinking LED lights. It has been set up to protect
the officials from the uncertain seasonal weather. There is Salwa
Akhannouch, radiant in a light Chanel-type tweed suit. Next to her
are a representative of the Al Jedaie group, with a moustache and
a red keffiyeh, and a Moroccan general in uniform. On a prominent easel just to the right of the entrance, a photo of the king,
Mohammed VI, represents the extent of national pride at play.

These animated images from a web archive, that show these
two Arab women in modern dress opening the way for a cortège
of relatively important men, produce the incongruous feeling
of a half-hearted victory on a terrain of no importance. Perched
on platform shoes with stiletto heels, Lalla Meryem and Salwa
Akhannouch wobble along the gleaming floors of the new shopping centre. In the central hall, which has been decked out for
the occasion as a concert hall, they and their courtiers attend a
show consisting of a series of performances that are more or less
artistic, including one in which divers unfurl the Moroccan flag in
the country's biggest aquarium, among some three thousand fish
that are probably scared to death.

I don't know if Lalla Meryem stayed on for the Jennifer Lopez
concert that evening before a crowd of nouveau-riche spectators, joined by a few celebrities with diverse pedigrees such as
Bar Refaeli, Clive Owen, Farida Khelfa, and François-Henri Pinault.
Jennifer Lopez apparently charges a million dollars for a private

concert, a figure that tells us something about the ambitions, the means, the networks, and the determination of Salwa Idrissi Akhannouch.

In 2014, she and her minister husband achieved position number 1,210 in the world list of 1,675 billionaires that *Forbes* magazine has established. The wealth accumulated by this Amazigh power couple today totals about 1.5 billion dollars, placing them in eighteenth position for great fortunes in Africa and in third position in Morocco.

◌ I spend hours in my hotel room, unable to force my body to return to the shopping centre. On the top floor of the hotel is a hammam, open by appointment. The humid heat in which the hostess lets me bathe does not warm me up. I feel profoundly cold, out of reach of the steam that only softens my skin.

When the hostess rubs me down with a horsehair glove, fat rolls of dead skin drop to the damp marble floor. The long, powerful movements are making me shed. I am losing matter, I am flayed, I am reduced.

Casablanca feels hostile. I will not reach out.

◌ In the first months of operation, security guards screened visitors at the entrance to Morocco Mall, rejecting those who weren't sufficiently well-dressed in the name of security for the local elite and the foreign shoppers who were the mall's actual targets. From the beginning, all the prices in the mall were set unreasonably high, doubtless instigated by some holder of an MBA, who we can imagine expounding the theory he has learned by heart about how to position prices (basically, the more expensive it is, the more desirable it will be).

When the mall opened, Aksal said it expected to see 20 percent foreign clientele in its annual goal of 14 million visitors—a figure some consultant obviously pulled out of a hat like a white rabbit. Armed with his calculator, he would have emphasized the fact that

Casa's airport is the main point of entry to the country, and with its 7 million passengers per year, 40 percent of these (give or take) should be ready—either before or after a low-cost flight averaging two and a half hours—to travel fifteen minutes down the road to relax in front of an American blockbuster, drink a banana milkshake, or take a selfie with the fish in the kingdom's biggest aquarium. In 2014, the Morocco Mall website was still providing schedules for shuttles connecting the shopping centre to the best hotels in Casa. But this shuttle service was soon abandoned for lack of business.

I don't know how long it took for Aksal to realize that Casa may be a city of 3 million people, and certainly the least poor in Morocco, but its "middle class" earns no more than 3,500 to 5,300 dirhams per month (330 to 500 euros). This income may, in a best-case scenario, allow someone to be well-dressed enough to enter Morocco Mall, but once inside, that person cannot afford even a plain coffee, for 15 dirhams.

In the first quarter of 2016, Galeries Lafayette closed shop. The luxurious 10,000-square-metre space, plated in fake gold and listed in the *Guinness Book of World Records*, is now partially inhabited by Tati, the iconic low-cost fuchsia-coloured French company whose Moroccan franchise was acquired by Aksal just before it went bankrupt. The rest of the space is occupied by Zara Home and Maisons du Monde.

◌ Arrogance, hubris, blind ambition, or naïveté? Salwa Akhannouch belongs to the segment of the population figuring in the last percentile of the income distribution curve, people who will hardly realize how out of step their reality is with that of the other 99 percent.

Beyond the white walls and the lush vegetation that surround and protect her mansion in the California-style suburb of Casablanca, everyone else, including me, can see only the slums and the dust of Douar Laâtour. Salwa Akhannouch sees Paris, Dubai, Singapore, the ski slopes of Courchevel, and the American school for her children. Inside her limousine, her gaze fixed on the screen of her cellphone, she catches echoes of the world that isn't hers in the form of PowerPoint presentations that expensive consultants have slickly produced, providing dubious statistics that say exactly what she wants to hear.

Who can expect this woman to enter into a conversation with tourist X at Mohammed V International Airport and ask them if they really intend—before or after their seven-day tour of Fez, Marrakech, Ouarzazate, and Essaouira—to also tour the biggest Zara Home store in Africa?

"Build it big and they will come" is what Mohammed bin Rashid Al Maktoum, another specimen of this last percentile, said. Unlikely as it may seem, this is exactly what happened in the desert of Dubai. Maybe Salwa Akhannouch thinks she can free herself from the economic mediocrity of her fellow citizens; others have bet on this before her, and won.

◌ All three of them are tall. Athletic physiques, tight-fitting clothes. One of the two women is wearing gold-coloured running shoes with high heels. Behind the diamonds sparkling in his earlobes, the young man's freshly shaved head shows off the arabesques he must have asked his barber to cut with a razor. They've put their sunglasses back on for the selfie, all three of them with pouting lips, in front of the Gucci boutique. They are about twenty years old. The woman with the Vuitton handbag is the man's sister; the one with the golden shoes is his girlfriend.

Lagos is poorly equipped for the class of ultra-rich Nigerians these three obviously stem from. They are tourists here. Tomorrow they will be in London. You can find them on social media, raising their cocktail glasses under the multicoloured spotlights of some trendy nightclub or striking a silly pose with a statue that means nothing to them, trying on the hats of soccer fans in some other shopping centre, pouting with 3-D glasses and a bag of popcorn in front of a film poster advertising some American star.

Of course, they don't make up 2.8 million people. But my unexpected meeting with three examples of such tourists, who I was certain didn't exist, rather shakes my confidence.

⚬ The purpose of a mermaid in a big aquarium is to entertain the vast majority of visitors who don't know what to do with the austere information about marine ecology that is usually posted on these huge fish cages. The aquariums have given up justifying their absurd existence with a pseudo-educative function and have now turned to promoting the commonplaces of childhood fantasies in order to "drive traffic," to resort to the expression used when people post photos of cats on the internet. The aquarium mermaids are the cousins of the department store Santa Claus.

Claire Baudet is the first professional mermaid in France. She is not only a pretty young woman of twenty-five, with long blond hair and a good body, but she is also writing a thesis at the Sorbonne (intellectual support welcome), and she is a remarkable athlete, since as a mermaid she has to spend quite a long time holding her breath. She works regularly at the Paris Aquarium, but also exercises her talents in nightclubs and at the pool parties of Greek millionaires.

Twice already, Morocco Mall has brought Claire Baudet the Mermaid and her silicone tail from France to drive traffic. Hundreds of children and their parents were crowded around the nine-by-thirteen-metre column of water and stacked right to the uppermost galleries to watch the fake imaginary creature undulate her monofin and toss "kiss bubbles" to the beat of a Disney tune. Everyone could turn their back on her in order to take a photo of themselves not watching her, while Claire was on the other side of the reinforced plexiglass, making friendly gestures but not actually seeing the spectators either, even though her eyes were wide open. It is impossible for a human being inside an aquarium to distinguish anything on the outside unless they are wearing a mask or goggles (which does not take into account that—depending on the quality of the water, which may be questionable at Morocco Mall—a performance of this kind can burn the conjunctiva).

Thanks to Claire the Mermaid, but also to nine Saman dancers from Sumatra who came to promote tourism in Indonesia, several concerts by Moroccan pop stars, various talent and beauty contests, a Pokémon GO tournament, and the entire arsenal of promotional events that shopping centres can deploy in order to attract customers, Aksal can claim with a more or less clear conscience that in five years of activities, 80 million people have walked through the mall.

○ On an earlier trip to Morocco, in the souk in Rabat, I became friends with a merchant of Berber rugs because I agreed not to report him to the police for fraud. This man, with a biblical name, had sold me a gorgeous red and gold rug, one and a half by three metres, whose edges needed repair. He had promised to send it to the best upholsterer in the country and then on to me in Switzerland. But he lost all the money I left with him playing cards, didn't have enough to pay for the repairs, and so my rug was held hostage.

I resorted to Y., the merchant's son, who admitted with some shame that his father was in the process of wrecking the extraordinary potential of his business with his abuse of alcohol and gambling. Over the phone he told me his father had a special eye and a vast network in the south of the country as well as a business sense that was so remarkable he should have easily become rich. He has a good heart, the son said. I would just have to wait; the money would show up, and the rug too. A report to the police would have been the final straw for this family business that was already struggling and supporting seven people.

Right now, the rug is at my feet, adding a typically bourgeois-bohemian ethno-chic décor to the white furnishings in my office.

One day when Casablanca was getting me down with its grey weather, its ambitions, the institutionalized lies its media kept repeating, the injustice paving its streets, its ugliness, its submissiveness, the condition of "developing country" it embodies, I went to see Y. and his father.

I can't say why exactly Rabat is my favourite among all the cities I know in Morocco. Perhaps because its aura is one of calm nostalgia. There is no rush. In the last hours of this journey that has killed my taste for travel, the royal city offered me a retreat, like an admission of weakness.

Y. and I have stayed friends on Facebook. I have seen him support the Moroccan soccer team, post questionable humorous videos, circulate photos of heart-shaped cakes for Valentine's Day, marry a beautiful young woman, and become the father of an adorable little girl.

Every now and then he sends me photographs of the loveliest rugs his father has brought back from the south, rare pieces, carefully selected, valuable. He forwards these photos by email to all his clients, former tourists who visited his shop and with whom he maintains solid virtual contact.

The new generation of rug merchants is making notable use of social media. Freed from the limitations of time and space, borders and middlemen, this generation is developing an alternative style of business that is based on the simplest and most direct relationships, a style that is at once global and local.

Even if he had the chance to open a boutique at Morocco Mall for free, I am not sure Y. would choose to do so.

○ Heading home. Tossing out kilos of suddenly useless papers, flyers, press kits, chip packets, apple cores, empty cups, business cards of people I didn't like, the wax paper left over from a merguez sandwich, a dozen plastic bags—all into the hotel garbage bin.

Flinging the clothes whose smell I can't stand anymore into one suitcase along with all the electronics I won't be using anymore either. Swiping a hotel towel because that's the tradition, even though my heart's not in it.

I am leaving Casablanca in a state of psychic distress I could not have imagined. The hotel doorman, dressed like the Belgian cartoon character Spirou, takes charge of calling me a taxi while I wait at the entrance in a bad mood I no longer try to hide. For the last forty-eight hours I have given myself over to almost total silence. I can no longer tolerate anyone, including myself.

A world tour of oversized commerce, along with twenty-three days of continuous jet lag, is the cruellest thing one could wish on one's worst enemy. I guess I don't really like myself. Travelling in order to take the pulse of humanity at the mercy of the least enlightened liberalism imaginable is actually moral suicide. I no longer believe in anything, and I no longer see clearly either.

Casablanca Airport is the last straw.

LISBON

I AM NOT ON Air Portugal's TAP 954 flight to Geneva. A delay of two hours and forty-five minutes at the airport in Casablanca, for technical reasons everyone regrets but no one is responsible for, and I am not on the TAP 954 flight to Geneva.

It is 8:17 p.m. I am in Lisbon, 1,900 kilometres southwest of home. At this very moment a little boy is finishing his supper or, more likely, has set it aside to focus on his favourite activity with all the obsessive intensity of his two and a half years: commenting in his perky little voice on pages 44 to 47 of *L'Île Noire*, where Ranko the gorilla beats his chest and throws big rocks at Tintin and Milou. With him is a man whose scent and companionship I have come to miss more and more. He will put his son to bed in half an hour or so, then settle in a caramel-coloured club chair to watch a black-and-white movie on the video system in the living room.

I am not on the TAP 954 flight to Geneva, and everything drains out of me with my tears: the twenty-five time zones of the world I have crossed via unimagined territories, my physical exhaustion, the successive loss of my bags and of meaning, faith, inclination, words, and desire. I haven't reached Ithaca yet. A few more hours, not even one night; it is trembling like a fragile mirage before my teary eyes.

☼ I flake out on a row of seats in the airport. Backrests and seats are large square pieces of lightly stuffed vinyl in a dark blueish grey. The seats are held together by a polished steel structure, the same as in Beijing and Calgary. I am in a rectangular space, enclosed in glass and served by a Starbucks, in the middle of a series of structures that Vinci, the French conglomerate, built of recycled concrete in 2013.

I am not on the TAP 954 flight. I am imprisoned in a journey that doesn't want to come to an end, is beyond my control, wishes me dead by dilution in international commerce and final evaporation in conditioned air.

I tip my head back. I see myself in a huge mirror on the ceiling. I am that skinny, pale woman with the dark dry hair going white with age, her eyes red from stress. I am that rigid body, with bones protruding as my neck contorts. I am that lined face that doesn't tell you where it is from, not yesterday and not today, a face melded over the course of travel. I am Europe and Asia, or neither, an assemblage of stateless features, questioned wherever I go, without a clear origin.

In the mirror, two rows back, I see an upside-down reflection of an Asian woman and a little round-eyed girl. The little mixed-race girl is playing with a stuffed toy monkey, making it strike poses and attitudes. She gets up, she sits back down, she moves around, she's bored. Her mother watches her, gives her a hug, sets her on the seat beside her, kisses the top of her head. Now and then she stops time in order to catch a moment of it as a family memory: she uses her cellphone to take a photo of her daughter and then taps something into the screen. Mother and daughter are cheek to cheek, matching their high cheekbones, smiling into the phone held at arm's length, changing position, re-starting, re-smiling, this time with the toy monkey. Again the mother taps on the phone and the girl plays. I wonder if there is a father at the other end of the airwaves, receiving these images that document their crossing from one ever-smaller world to another place they are getting to know more and more.

◌ Travelling, going where they want. I watch them, mother and daughter. They could have a thousand reasons for being there. Tourism, exile, or reunion. Flight forward or back again. The waiting areas in airports, train stations, bus terminals, and ports are full of these desires for destinations that make suitcase wheels purr along and pushcarts overflow, desires that unfurl from one security check to the next, until it's time to board. Desires that move in clusters, in the air, on the sea, overland.

My first journey, at age three, was into exile. I was with my mother and we were moving to Switzerland. At the airport in Zurich a man was waiting for us. He would become my mother's husband and a father to me. I would bear his name. We had all met in Korea. I was born a few years earlier. Another man had loved my mother, but it didn't matter; we were going to be a family.

I have no memory of this first long-haul flight of my life. Which airline? What stopovers? My mother's apprehension, her excitement at this long trip that was also her first. We must have had a lot of baggage, but at the time the suitcase wheels didn't make the same noise. What did the airport at Gimpo, in the suburbs of Seoul, look like? I imagine we left from there, my mother and I in 1980, when South Korea was still a military dictatorship under American influence. How much time did it take to check documents, passports, exit visas, the countless authorizations acquired with patience, and perhaps contortions, from a recalcitrant, labyrinthine administration. Even recently it wasn't easy to get out of South Korea. At customs, what was the look on the face of the official, his uniform bursting with the self-importance this dinky power invested in him, as he assessed the single mother and her child, these worthless lives leaving for the other end of the world?

Airplanes haven't changed much since this first voyage, except for the smell of cigarette smoke that never bothered anyone. Maybe we flew in a jumbo jet, as they used to be called, and our trip must have taken more than twenty-four hours because at the time it was impossible to fly over China or Russia. Did we have a layover in the Middle East? In Dubai? Bahrain? Jeddah? The airports were not what they are today, and neither was air travel. Did we change planes, or did we just get off for the time it took to refuel? How much time did we spend waiting? I was three years old, my mother probably held my hand. We were halfway, in an airport in the desert with men wearing keffiyehs and dishdashas, exotic sights for our innocent eyes.

I now think my mother must have been afraid. Not of the men in their robes, but of the whole trip, what it meant and what was definitive and radical about it. Our cruising speed of 800 kilometres an hour created a distance of 8,800 kilometres between her and her father, her mother, her seven brothers and sisters, and her country, her mother tongue, her culture—in sum, between her and the world in which she was born, the only one she knew.

There were no cellphones or internet, and very few computers. International phone communications cost a fortune. Phone calls from Switzerland to Korea cost an arm and a leg. Globalization did not exist as it does today. There were borders, and prohibitive distances. You were not sure you would find an H&M, a Zara, or a Starbucks at the other end of your journey. Besides, what did my mother know about this Switzerland she was exiling herself to? Had she seen photos? How did she imagine it? Doubtless more modern than Korea, but that was not really a mental image she could project. So it didn't matter much. In Switzerland, people had democratic rights, freedom of the press, and clean air. Women like her, who were burdened with a little bastard child like me, weren't viewed as badly as they were in stiff, proud Korea where you don't fiddle with bloodlines. Still...she was on her way to Switzerland to get married. She was in love.

Travelling. I have often done it since. Back to Korea, coming, going, as often as possible. Then business trips, reporting. But the first trip, that I have no memory of, is the one that haunts me every day because it made me what I am. It inhabits me, or rather I still inhabit it, I relive it constantly. This journey is a part of all my journeys. I question it. I have unconsciously sought its traces and feelings in each of my subsequent journeys, in all parts of the world.

Maybe I have frequented airports the way salmon swim upriver. That must be my condition. I am discovering it as I write. In this month of January 2014, I went on a rather weird trip that I first devised in order to write a book. Travelling—not for pleasure, without a final destination, but with a fixed idea. A journey like a manifesto, a sort of pronouncement. But it may have been more of a deficit-journey, a failure of touristic proportions that I still need to grasp completely.

I close my eyes like you blow out a candle. Everything fades before the confused spiral of memory. When I reopen them and look in the mirror overhead, my reflection has disappeared.

Other Titles from University of Alberta Press

How to Clean a Fish
And Other Adventures in Portugal
ESMERALDA CABRAL
An extended family stay in Portugal, full of food, adventure, and the search for home.
Wayfarer Series

Blue Portugal and Other Essays
THERESA KISHKAN
Braided essays about the natural world, aging bodies, family histories, and art and visual phenomena.
Wayfarer Series

Tiny Lights for Travellers
NAOMI K. LEWIS
Vulnerable and funny, this award-winning memoir explores Jewish identity, family, the Holocaust, and belonging.
Wayfarer Series

More information at uap.ualberta.ca